us!

Hope for remission of LS symptoms via natural healing methods

including Sodium tetraborate (borax) therapies

Collated wisdom from fellow sufferers

Allicia Mae Cain & Ann Foweraker

HELP! I Have Lichen Sclerosus!
Hope for remission of LS symptoms
via natural healing methods
including Sodium tetraborate (borax) therapies
Collated wisdom from fellow sufferers
Allicia Mae Cain & Ann Foweraker

ISBN: 978-1-909936-28-7

Set in Gentium Book Basic

Paperback edition ii Pendown Publishing
Cornwall UK 2020
Pendownpublishing.co.uk

Cover: PP Designs

p. **HELP - I have Lichen Sclerosus ...**

5 **Ch 1: Up Front**

7 **Ch 2: What is Lichen Sclerosus?**

13 **Ch 3: OUR LS Stories**

20 **Ch 4: What is Borax?**

22 **Ch 5: Is Borax Safe?**

33 **Ch 6: Ways to use Borax**

46 **Ch 7: Magnesium & Other supplements**

54 **Ch 8: Borax / Steroid / or Both? And what about vulval cancer?**

58 **Ch 9: Other Natural Remedies**

60 **Ch 10: Fusing/Absorption/Agglutination/ Atrophy/Adhesion/Scarring/Bruising**

65 **Ch 11: Flares, Triggers and how to manage them**

76 **Ch 12: Sex Life / Pregnancy**

80 **Ch 13: What to Wear or Use Down There**

83 **Ch 14: Problems concerning urination or defecation**

87 **Ch 15: Lichen Sclerosus in MEN & Notes on LS in Children**

90 **Ch 16: Commercial Lotions and Potions**

93 **Ch 17: Skin condition terms it is useful to know**

96 **Ch 18: LS and Other Auto Immune conditions**

97 **APPENDIX 1 Where in the world to buy borax**

98 **APPENDIX 2 You are not alone - where to find the LS community and support**

100 **For your own notes**

This book is dedicated to all the wonderful, amazing, and resourceful people we have met only because we all happen to suffer from this chronic condition - may we all find relief

Ch 1: Up Front

Up Front
You don't have to buy this book - there is lots of information out there in internet land - but finding it *(if it is still there)* and sifting it out of the tangle of threads that come and go on a daily basis - ***that is hard.***

We have written what we would have liked to find when we first heard that we had Lichen Sclerosus (LS)

What you will not find here:
You will not find a medical opinion - we are not doctors.

We are just people who have LS, know what it is to SUFFER with it, know what it is like to try using the prescribed solutions - and know that there are other ways to control the symptoms - and are both currently in remission through these 'other ways'.

What you will find in here:
Collated wisdom from us, and over 4000 other suffers in the LS community.
Information about LS: remedies and methods, diet, stress, clothing, lotions, potions and support.
How to locate specific scientific papers relating to: LS, properties of borax, data and research.

This book aims to show you natural methods, and especially borax therapies in detail, for controlling the symptoms of LS to the point of remission.
By remission, we mean that 90 – 95% of the time you are not experiencing the worst symptoms - the

itching, soreness, swelling or tearing. That other aspects are improving or, at least, not getting any worse – like fusing or skin-thinning. That when a flare hits it can, reasonably quickly, be brought under control.

We are not anti medical solutions, nor are we anti-steroid - however, we know that the medical profession do not have all the answers, that some do not know much about this condition and that steroids do not work, or cease to work, for ***some*** people.

This book also aims to inform about Lichen Sclerosus, the location and the factors that affect the way it presents, address some of the big and worrying questions and give useful information about what other aspects of daily life can support remission.

We aim only to inform and give options - so that people can do their own research and make their own informed choices.

Ch 2: What is Lichen Sclerosus?

What is LS?

The most basic description should be: Lichen Sclerosus (also called Lichen Sclerosis) is a chronic inflammatory skin disorder affecting both females *and* males of *any* age.
However, as you are here reading this book, you probably know what Lichen Sclerosus *is* – even if your doctor didn't tell you – you will probably have Googled it and got a full and baffling description already. (Go to Ch 17: Skin Condition Terms, towards the end of this book for a more detailed definition).

Let us highlight what it is NOT

It is NOT contagious / catching.
You cannot get LS from sexual or other contact.
It is nothing to do with the plant 'lichen'. The name Lichen is given because, basically, the plaques that the skin forms *look* like a flat lichen (like those that grow on rocks) It has **no relationship** whatsoever to the plant Lichen, or to fungi either *(lichen, the plant, being a symbiotic relationship between and algae and a fungi).*
Sclerosus/sclerosis just means hardening/ thickening (from thickening due to scarring or other skin changes) though, ironically, Lichen Sclerosus also results in thinning of the skin – it was the thickening that seems to have been incorporated into the name.

What causes LS?
Its cause is not completely known or understood.

It is thought to be an auto-immune condition - scientific evidence for this is building.

There is an hereditary element in some people. This may be related to skin-type or other sensitivities that are also hereditary by one mechanism or other. Before dismissing hereditary elements it is worth remembering that many women would not have spoken about this condition if they had it in times past (or if elderly now even) due to embarrassment or social taboos, and so maybe not even have consulted a doctor - so, unless you ask your family members you may not know if there is a family connection.

There is a strong link to oestrogen levels in some people - as in pre-menstrual or menopausal.

It can also arrive ‘out of the blue’ – no direct relatives with the condition, no oestrogen issues, no drugs implicated, no other autoimmune conditions present.

It can be a (rare) side-effect to certain prescribed medications – and noted in the medication information sheet as such.

It is often found in people who suffer from other autoimmune conditions.

As with other auto-immune conditions – it may be related to ‘leaky-gut’ or a disrupted micro-biome.

Who can suffer from LS?

There appears to be an element to presenting with LS that is controlled by the amount of oestrogen in the

body – as it is more common in pre-pubescent girls and post-menopausal women.
However, it does occur, more frequently than most doctors would have us believe, in women of all ages. So much so that women between pre-pubescent and menopause are frequently misdiagnosed with other conditions before it is finally accepted that it is LS.
Moreover, LS also occurs in boys and men, though to a lesser extent.

Is it really 'rare'?
When you are diagnosed you may be told that the condition is rare – or relatively rare. This is probably not the case as it is a very under reported condition – as most vulval /vaginal conditions are - especially where it is culturally taboo to talk about the genital area of your body.

One study predicted that it was likely to be at least 60% under-reported in females. It is less likely to be under reported in males as it is more visible and the cultural taboos do not apply in the same way. Even so – it *is* reported by 1% of the population – that is a huge number of people suffering this condition. It is also considered the most common of the inflammatory conditions of the vulva. *(The vulva is not the vagina)*

Naming the parts - and why
One of the most important things about going to speak with a medical professional about your genital area is the naming of parts. It is important - as saying that you are sore 'in your vaginal area' when you meant your 'vulva' would result in the doctor thinking you have a different condition – and, possibly, treating the

wrong condition. If this sounds far-fetched, we have to tell you – from reports we have read - it is not!

Cloak yourself with knowledge before you speak to the medical professional. Use the correct terms – it can also help distract from embarrassment and give you both a clear handle on what you are talking about.

DIAGRAM for women.

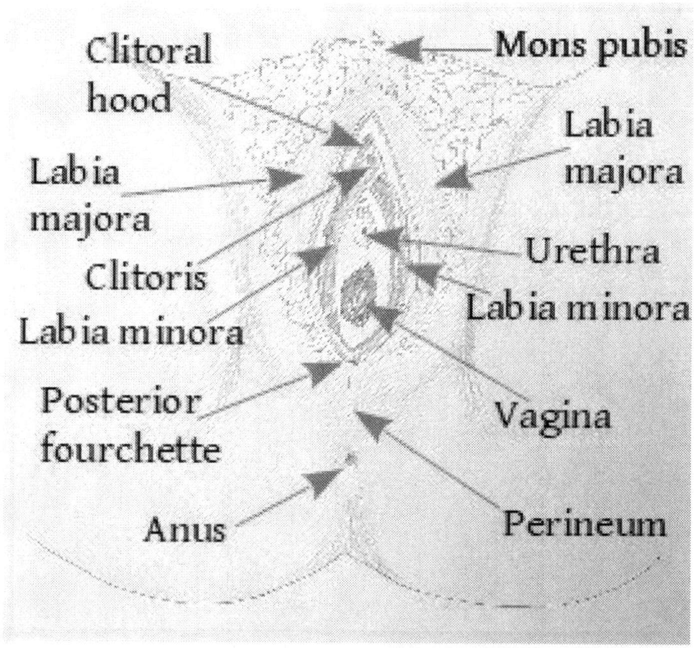

(Note - Chapter 15 deals with Men and LS)

Check it out!

Not only you - but also if you have daughters (or daughters-in-law) girlfriends, aunts, cousins ... do encourage them to get to know what their vulva looks like - and to examine it manually and visually once a month - rather like doing your own breast examination - it can pick up the first signs of something going wrong. We have heard so many women say that by the time they looked, the changes were so far gone they didn't know what their own vulva *should* have looked like in the first place. And note, we are all different in this department. No one vulva looks identical to another. As a visual aid search on the internet for 'the labia library' or 'one hundred vulvas - an artwork Laura Dodsworth' - or even 'Jamie McCartney - artwork vulva casts' - and you will see what we mean. *(even if the media insist of calling their work 'vaginas')*

If you want to know what Lichen Sclerosus looks like - the best thing is to look on the internet under images. There are also medical information pages which have full colour pictures of LS affected vulvas and penises in all stages of the condition. For an extreme view - do a search for the video 'bsccp lichens of the vulva video' for a medical overview with extreme cases requiring serious medical intervention *- though maybe not for the squeamish or the easily worried.*

Make a record:

One thing we really wished we had done - was to make and keep a photographic record of our LS as it progressed. This helps in giving evidence when talking to doctors, and it helps you monitor any changes.
The best way is to take 'vulva selfies' and then to store

them somewhere safe. There are 'photo vaults' available where *only you* can access your photos, or you can download them onto a USB / memory stick, - which *you keep only* for your LS photos and notes - and then delete them from *everywhere* else.

How LS is diagnosed:
Diagnosis can take a while as many ordinary doctors do not see Lichen Sclerosus often enough to identify it easily – which is why, we guess, they consider it rare. In the meantime you may be prescribed antibiotics, anti-fungal creams, treated for yeast infections, suggested that it is a STI or even told it is just an irritant from a soap or shampoo and the suggestion to try something hypoallergenic.
A dermatologist or a gynaecologist may have a better idea of what they are looking at. However, it can be identified by an experienced doctor visually – but sometimes a biopsy is required as LS does not present itself identically in all people and can be confused with other conditions.

How LS is usually treated by doctors (and the problems with this approach)
Once a diagnosis has been made the usual treatment is a steroid cream or ointment. The particular variety may vary, but it is usually a strong (potent) steroid. Clobetasol (also sold as Dermovate) is a common brand used, it is a type of **Corticosteroid.**
The *typical* instruction is to use this on the affected area once a day for two weeks (a pea sized amount) thereafter reducing to once every two days and then after another two weeks, twice a week – for life. This is expected to keep the symptoms away.

Ch 3: OUR LS Stories

As we have stated - we both suffer from Lichen Sclerosus – so we bring you our LS stories. Yours will, most probably, not be exactly the same, but that doesn't matter – each and every one of us is different. If nothing else has become obvious in the past few years, then the recognition that our bodies are so much more than we, and the scientific and medical fraternity, used to believe. When we now know that our gut bacteria can influence everything from our immune reactions to our mental health, it is clear that we are an organism with infinite variety in our make-up and therefore in our reactions to our environment.

Ann's Story:

{Ann lives in the UK}

Around September 2011, age 57, and two years into menopause, I began to get a persistent itch in the peri-anal region. I first thought it was a reaction to something like a shampoo or a soap (running down and between my buttocks). My skin has 'always' been sensitive. I say 'always' as I can't tell you what it was like when a young child, but I can say it was sensitive from about ten as I know that certain things would react with my skin. Like metals, other than gold and silver, or the way my skin would get sore in contact with some types of thread or over-react to small bites or stings.

I didn't go to the doctor to begin with as I first blamed the soap / shampoo - despite the fact that I had not changed the type of shampoo or soap at all – I suspected that the manufacturers had changed the ingredients. So I tried not using one or the other, using different 'hypoallergenic' versions instead.

Nothing changed, the itch grew worse and seemed to be spreading higher between my buttocks and further forward. I made an appointment, saw the doctor, who didn't know what it was – but prescribed an antibiotic – saying that if it worked it would still take a while for the irritation to subside.

It didn't work. I waited, to give it a good chance to work. I probably waited longer than necessary – but eventually I made another appointment, and I struck lucky, as the doctor I saw next had been a hospital dermatologist before turning to General Practice. She recognised the condition immediately, prescribed a corticosteroid cream and gave me instructions for its use, saying that I would have to use it for life. She also told me that it was an auto-immune condition and that, sadly, it could not be cured, only managed. I was not asked to go back for any follow-up and I went on my way.

I was a compliant patient. I followed the 'rules' of application to the letter ... and it seemed to work. The itching subsided, the whiter areas seemed to go - it was still sore however. I had stopped riding my bicycle before the diagnosis, and I still couldn't ride it again in comfort.

Gradually, over the next four years, the efficacy of the corticosteroid began to wear off – I was advised to 'start the procedure again' to do two weeks of twice a day, two weeks of once a day and then back to just

twice a week. It made no difference ... I had been told there was nothing else doctors could prescribe.
After about eight months of excruciating pain – I couldn't sit down for more than half an hour, it was too painful (difficult when you are an author!) - I was desperate. My mirror showed me that the skin between my buttocks was shiny red, severely swollen, blistered and cracked. The perineum and the vulva were patchy, greyish-white and red, and sore - and my labia minora had apparently shrunk dramatically.

At this point I said to myself – well, I know I was told it was auto-immune and incurable – and that there is only the potent steroid for treatment – but I'm going to look to see if there is *anything* else out there – something natural perhaps.

I have a bit of a scientific background. I know what I am looking for in evidence. If I read something I will not take it on face value – I seek out the original sources – and so I approached this search in the same way.

At one point I found the information about LS and Borax. I set to - following up on every scientific claim that the article mentioned ... and then on the ones mentioned within those. (Ways to find many of these are included in Ch 5)
I came to the conclusion that there would be no harm in trying the borax baths – and found a supplier. (See Appendix 1: Where in the World to buy Borax)

As is documented in my Author Blog *(which I already had on annfoweraker.com)* I tried the bath, a shallow

bath, in a full-sized bath tub, with a tablespoon of Borax and a tablespoon of bicarbonate of soda.
It was amazing! The relief from the itch - immediate ... and it lasted for awhile even after I got out of the bath.
I went on to try the ingesting method - as described in detail on my blog post 'Lichen Sclerosus and why Borax is my new best friend' - and in the 'Up-Date on LS and Borax' post.

Within a fortnight my skin was pink again, blister-free – the swelling was reduced and the soreness gone away.
I couldn't believe it!
I continued the ingesting – now on the maintenance dose (which it says you need to continue for life) and also with my daily borax soaks in a shallow bath – just 10 minutes a day, but even this I sometimes missed a day ... or two.

I also started using Borax as my shampoo – and blogged about that long before I had the courage to blog about its effect on my LS. I still couldn't quite believe it ... but after four months **I decided to go public – to tell the world.**

Being so public about my LS was a hard thing to do – **but, I reasoned, if only one woman found it helped – then my 'embarrassment' would be worth it.**
That was February 2017.

Allicia's Story: *{Allicia lives in the USA}*

When I was in my early 30's I got an email from my mother that said that her gynaecologist asked her to email me and my sister and tell us that she had been diagnosed with something called Lichen Sclerosus and that sometimes it runs in families and we should know that we may be at risk. I asked her what it was and she said she really didn't know. She didn't even really know she had it and the gynaecologist had just noticed it during her exam. She said she had some fusing, but hadn't noticed anything otherwise herself. The gynaecologist gave her a series of steroid shots in her private area and also gave her a steroid cream to put on the area. I remember googling Lichen Sclerosus and thinking that it was some kind of skin condition that you had and you treated it and it eventually went away.

In my late 30's I started to have an itchy spot at the top of my clitoris and it would come and go. I really didn't pay too much attention to it. It very slowly got progressively worse. My husband developed a gambling addiction and, due to this, we started to have marriage problems. During this time the itching got really bad and my vulva skin started turning white and I started to get little sores on it. I started wondering if maybe I had Lichen Sclerosus. At this point I got on online and started doing a lot of research and I was convinced that I had Lichen Sclerosus.

I made an appointment with my gynaecologist and asked her to take a look. I told her that I thought I had

Lichen Sclerosus and she said, 'What's that?' I had to tell her what it was and she scheduled me for a biopsy. My biopsy came back positive and she gave me a prescription for a steroid cream and a cream for yeast infection. She basically sent me on my way and really never gave me any explanation as to what I had or even how to treat it.

I used the steroid cream and it seemed to help. I thought that I would use up my tube of steroid cream and it would clear everything up and my vulva would go back to normal.

A few months later I went through a knee surgery from a car accident injury.
Then I lost my house because of my husband's gambling - and then we went through a divorce.
Right after that my Lichen Sclerosus symptoms got really out of control. I had irritation and burning 24/7 for months and months.
The steroid cream had stopped working and I soon realized that it was making me worse and it was burning my skin and causing big welts. I began searching for natural remedies to treat my condition.

The first thing I tried was Emuaid, which I loved so much and still use to this day. I still felt like I needed something more. I had started dating the man who is now my husband and I knew I wanted to get healthy for myself, but also for my new sex life. I spent hours and days and months looking for answers, when one day my life changed.

I found a blog written by Ann Foweraker. She had just written her blog and she also had Lichen Sclerosus and she was talking about using borax.

The first thing that came to my mind was the stuff my grandma used in her laundry.

There was just something almost magical for me when I read Ann's blog. I went immediately to the store and bought my first box of borax - **and my life was totally changed** - through soaking in, and ingesting, borax.

I went on to form a Borax for LS support group on Facebook to share the good news as much as possible. This group was supporting over 4,000 ladies when one day, for no reason, it vanished. Repeated requests from myself, and distraught members, gained no insight into why this happened.

There was nothing for it but to start again. My new group 'Sharing is Caring about Lichen Sclerosus et al' grows everyday - and the collective wisdom and the knowing that you are not alone is welcomed by all who join.

However, aware that all this could so easily vanish at the whim of an anonymous Facebook bot, Ann and I decided to gather together all we knew, particularly about the borax therapies, to provide help and support that is available in a more permanent way - and create this book.

Ch 4: What is Borax?

For many the term 'borax' calls up pictures of mother's laundry day. For others it is not something seen or heard of anymore.

Borax is NOT a laundry detergent. It is used with detergents to get a better wash, probably because it is alkaline and therefore helps the soap work up.

It is also used as an insecticide (against ants), as flux in blacksmithing work, as a component in glass and ceramics, in many household cleaning products, in many cosmetics and hair or skin-care products (as preservative, emulsifier or pH regulator) and in contact-lens solution.

Borax IS a mineral - mined, predominantly, in California and Turkey.

It's chemical name is Sodium tetraborate or Sodium tetraborate decahydrate or Sodium borate.
It is the chemical salt of boron – and basically reacts with the hydrochloric acid in your stomach to release boron directly into your system if you ingest it.

In appearance it is a white, crystalline, finely-gritty substance – it dissolves in hot water, though often leaving some tiny gritty bits.

Unless it has been mixed with something else (perfumes / colours etc) it is 99.9% pure in the form that you can buy it in as 20 Mule Team Borax – or the equivalent from Turkey. 'Food grade' is just the same.

IT IS **NOT** BORAX ***SUBSTITUTE*** – DO NOT USE THIS AT ALL!

IT is **NOT** BORIC ACID – this has other uses – but not for LS.

It is NOT BORON – this is the ingredient we want if we ingest it – but it is more accessible to our bodies if taken as the chemical salt version – sodium tetraborate. Boron is important for health, but most people will be low in boron as industrially grown foods are usually low in boron as the soil has been depleted of boron by dependency on artificial fertilizers.

If you go on the internet - or even if you are member of some LS groups - you will see many warnings against using Borax - *some* of these even seem authoritative ...
so why did we still go ahead and use it?

Ch 5: Is Borax Safe?

Yes - you will see many warnings against using Borax

This is what the warnings say:
They say borax is toxic.
They say it may cause fertility problems.
They say it is an irritant.

Let's have a closer look.
(All EVIDENCE is in the footnotes which are to be found at the end of this chapter)

Toxicity:

BORAX and TABLE SALT have roughly the same degree of toxicity. (Footnotes 1 & 2)

Neither salt nor borax would you ingest knowingly to the degree needed to prove to be toxic – or even make you feel ill.
That said – it should be labelled and placed away from children – as, we think, should large quantities of salt – taken that just a ***teaspoon*** of **table-salt** killed a 17-month child in 2016.

The level of borax taken for LS:
The amounts to take are very, very small. (Precise details in Ch 6)
The highest dose (for women) in any protocols works out at 500mg (a boron dose of about 56mg/day) for a whole woman! (The LD (lethal dose) would be 3000 milligrams (mg) **per KILO of a person's weight**!)

Then, the life-time (maintenance) dose drops to 30 mg of borax per day, giving a boron dose of 3mg/day, which is the recommended amount to benefit from the many positives listed in the Abstract 'Nothing Boring About Boron' **(Footnote 3).**

Fertility problems:

The studies that showed this used *rats and mice* and used **very high doses of boric acid** (in levels that would make a human feel sick (nauseous) if scaled up) – and certain fertility and embryo growth problems were noted.

However ...
The **human** studies* have shown **no fertility problems.** *With significant numbers from the population of workers in the borax mining and boric-acid production facilities with high and long-term exposure to sodium borates. **(Footnotes 4 & 5)** These seem more reliable as evidence for humans.

As an Irritant:

As a **powder**, it could be considered an irritant – mainly to the eyes - however, at no time is it suggested that anyone would use borax in powder form for LS, it is always dissolved.
Even so – the evidence is lacking for irritation elsewhere - apart from the eyes - and that applies to **any** granular material.

Then consider the fact that Sodium borate is in the lens solution for contact lenses - which are taken from it and put straight onto the eye.

Side-effect Comparison:
One might ask – how does Borax compare to the most-used steroid for side-effects?

Footnote 6 is a precis from the patient's information for one of the most commonly prescribed potent steroid used for LS – for the recommended dose.

We can't help noticing that some of the side-effects listed (especially under 'more common', and 'less common') seem similar to those we suffer with, just from the LS – let alone adding to it!

As for the side-effects of borax, at the levels in the protocols designed to result in a dose of 3 mg of boron, please read the list in **Footnote 3 – they are all positive,** and please do look at the actual paper ***'Nothing Boring About Boron Lara Pizzorno'*** *published on PubMed (NCBI US National Library of Medicine. National Institutes of Health.)*

So, how do Borax and the most commonly prescribed steroids compare for safety and side-effects? You can decide.

The History of the Ban on Borax:

If you have read all this, and the footnotes so far, you might be confused as to why Borax has been banned in so many places in the world. There is a history to this – and it involves Dr Rex Newnham and the vested interest of the pharmaceutical companies.
For the best and easiest-to-find explanation we will refer you to look up **'The Borax Conspiracy – Walter Last'** on the internet. There you will find a full

explanation in an article by Walter Last. *It's an incredible story ... so ...*

Our first question was – is it true?

Having found published scientific papers on the use of boron and borax by Dr. Rex Newnham (PhD, DO, ND) and a published copy of a lecture he gave where he explained exactly what happened with his cure for arthritis (which used borax) – and found it is as Walter Last has reported in The Borax Conspiracy – we feel satisfied that *it is true!* **(Footnote 7)**

Can you use Borax if you have had a diagnosis of oestrogen sensitive Breast cancer?

This is a question that seems to come up now and again in the group – not least for Ann who has had a lumpectomy for breast cancer and is on an oestrogen blocker.

The good news is that, according to scientific papers, Borax (Boron) is safe for women who have had breast cancer, are oestrogen positive and on oestrogen blockers.

Lara Pizzorno – author of the scientific paper 'Nothing Boring about Boron' says - To Quote:

"If you need to be on an aromatase inhibitor, the good news is that not only will taking boron NOT interfere with the cancer protective effect of aromatase inhibitor therapy, but boron will lessen some of its harmful effects on your bones. Boron is still going to help you convert vitamin D into the form in which it helps absorb calcium most effectively and the latest research which I have discussed earlier in this series on boron is showing us that boron plays a number of protective roles for us including greatly lessening

chronic inflammation, which would otherwise excessively activate osteoclasts."
To read this further **search** *'Lara Pizzorno Boron and Breast Cancer'* to see the article on the AlgaeCal website, where she lists her scientific references.

In Conclusion

You must realise that, sadly, those who say that Borax is toxic are often only reading the headlines, they will not have done any in-depth research or are just giving the standard answer - and thereby covering themselves if you choose to ignore them. We highly recommend that you do your own IN-DEPTH research, by which we mean reading scientific papers and always checking conflicts of interest and sources.

EVIDENCE FOOTNOTES

Toxicity:

It used to be easy to look up Toxicity and other concerns on the US government site TOXNET - unfortunately they have decided to separate Toxnet out under many other websites according to uses - and in doing so have also taken away much of the research data that the statements were based on. However, if you want to check search for Toxnet then follow the instructions to find the new location and search HSDB (Health and Safety Data Bank) under the new headings, to enter the substances searched.

FOOTNOTE 1) Sodium Chloride – Table Salt
The estimated **fatal** dose (LD = lethal dose) of sodium chloride is approximately 0.75g to **3 grams per kilogram of person's weight.**
Symptoms of poisoning: Nausea, diarrhea, rashes, central nervous system depression, and coma.
(Note: these are the symptoms of any sodium salt poisoning)
CASE: An estimated dose of more than 400 mEq/kg resulted in brain injury and death in a 2 year old child given a salt water solution to induce emesis.
Dart, R.C. (ed). Medical Toxicology. Third Edition, Lippincott Williams & Wilkins. Philadelphia, PA. 2004., p. 1057

FOOTNOTE 2) Sodium Tetraborate - Borax:
Estimated **fatal** dose (LD) is approximately (3000mg) **3 grams per kilogram of person's weight.**
CASE: An **intravenous** dose of 14-20 grams of sodium borate was administered for the purposes of neutron capture therapy to 10 patients, who experienced immediate nausea, vomiting, defecation, and occasionally seizures and respiratory depression.
Locksley HB, Farr LE; J Pharm Exp Ther 114: 484-9 (1955) as cited in Baselt RC; Biological Monitoring Methods for Industrial Chemicals p.50 (1980)

FOOTNOTE 3) Below: The 'Abstract' from the NCBI PubMed site: search 'Nothing Boring About Boron Lara Pizzorno'. The whole paper is free to read – the abstract below just shows the results from the study - which cites all the relevant scientific papers that support these assertions.

Abstract from 'Nothing Boring About Boron'

“ The trace mineral boron is a micronutrient with diverse and vitally important roles in metabolism that render it necessary for plant, animal, and human health, and as recent research suggests, possibly for the evolution of life on Earth. As the current article shows, boron has been proven to be an important trace mineral because it:
(1) is essential for the growth and maintenance of bone;
(2) greatly improves wound healing;
(3) beneficially impacts the body's use of estrogen, testosterone, and vitamin D;
(4) boosts magnesium absorption;
(5) reduces levels of inflammatory biomarkers, such as high-sensitivity C-reactive protein (hs-CRP) and tumor necrosis factor α (TNF-α);
(6) raises levels of antioxidant enzymes, such as superoxide dismutase (SOD), catalase, and glutathione peroxidase;
(7) protects against pesticide-induced oxidative stress and heavy-metal toxicity;
(8) improves the brains electrical activity, cognitive performance, and short-term memory for elders;
(9) influences the formation and activity of key biomolecules, such as S-adenosyl methionine (SAM-e) and nicotinamide adenine dinucleotide (NAD(+));
(10) has demonstrated preventive and therapeutic effects in a number of cancers, such as prostate, cervical, and lung cancers, and multiple and non-Hodgkin's lymphoma; and
(11) may help ameliorate the adverse effects of traditional chemotherapeutic agents.
In none of the numerous studies conducted to date,

however, do boron's beneficial effects appear at intakes less than 3 mg/day.
No estimated average requirements (EARs) or dietary reference intakes (DRIs) have been set for boron - only an upper intake level (UL) of 20 mg/d for individuals aged ≥ 18 y. The absence of studies showing harm in conjunction with the substantial number of articles showing benefits support the consideration of boron supplementation of 3 mg/d for any individual who is consuming a diet lacking in fruits and vegetables or who is at risk for or has osteopenia; osteoporosis; osteoarthritis (OA); or breast, prostate, or lung cancer." Lara Pizzorno

Fertility:

FOOTNOTE 4) In ncbi.nlm.nih.gov/pmc/articles. Search for *"Reproductive effects of sodium borates on male employees: birth rate assessment. M D Whorton, J L Haas, L Trent, and O Wong." 1994*

This study wanted to investigate any reproductive effects of exposure to high levels of sodium borate in humans. They studied the work-force of a large mining and production plant in the Mojave desert, California.
Using the standardised birth ratio they assessed the fertility for the male employees. They counted the number of births and the male to female ratio.
They explain the methods that they used to get a representational cross-section of the employees, to avoid bias and their methods of follow-up.
They reported a higher than average birth rate to usual, and a slightly higher number of female to male birth ratio over the, >30 years, of the study.

Their conclusion: “Under the conditions studied, **there were no adverse reproductive effects of high borate doses** as reported from oral ingestion studies in animals" *(Quote from the Abstract)*

NOTE: A much newer study *(Search: An overview of male reproductive studies of boron with an emphasis on studies of highly exposed Chinese workers. Oct 2020)* involving 1000 Chinese workers in sodium borate industries in Liaoning province in Northeast China and more precise methods – has also reported no effect on fertility.

FOOTNOTE 5) In pubmed.ncbi.nlm.nih.gov. **Seach** for: "Reproductive toxicity in boron exposed workers in Bandirma, Turkey. Nursen Basaran 1, Yalçin Duydu, Hermann M Bolt.”
These researchers began with stating that sodium borates have been said to be toxic to reproduction – because of the results from experiments on animals using very high doses.
However, they noted that this had not been shown in any epidemiological studies so far. They set out to investigate any reproductive toxicity in humans by studying those who have a high exposure to sodium borates due to their employment in a boric acid production plant in Bandirma, Turkey. *(Sodium borate is processed to make Boric acid)* There were 204 workers in the study. Their blood samples showed they had a high blood boron concentration. At the end of their study they concluded that: “Unfavorable effects of boron exposure on the reproductive toxicity indicators were **not** observed.” *(Quote from the Abstract)*

Side-effect Comparison:

(To compare with FOOTNOTE 3)

FOOTNOTE 6) Typical patient information for a steroid like those most frequently prescribed for LS.
For the Consumer:
Along with its needed effects, *this corticosteroid* may cause some unwanted effects. Although not all of these side effects may occur, if they do occur they may need medical attention.
Check with your doctor immediately if any of the following side effects occur while taking *this corticosteroid*.

They go on to say that burning or stinging where applied is 'more common', but that a feeling of burning to the skin, flushing or redness of the skin, soreness swelling, irritation, scaly-ness, a rash, oozing, itching and thinning with easy bruising, particularly where the skin folds together - come under 'less common'. Plus much, much more in less varying degrees of effect.

It is easy to see the full lists in the internet, Search for 'Patient Information sheets for **steroid name** For the Consumer' and if you like more information 'Healthcare Professionals information sheets **steroid name** *whichever steroid you have been prescribed*.

So, how do Borax and the most often prescribed steroid compare for side-effects? Have a look at the full details and then you can decide.

History of the Ban on Borax:

FOOTNOTE 7)

Do check out the cited *'The Borax Conspiracy - Walter Last'*, scrolling down to 'The Arthritis Cure of Rex Newnham', to understand the lengths that pharmaceutical companies will go to, to protect their profits.

To find a representative paper by Dr Rex Newnham see this one presented at the **International Symposium on Health Effects of Boron and Its Compounds** held 16-17 September 1992 at the University of California, Irvine, California. Search on the internet for **'Essentiality of Boron for Healthy Bones and Joints Rex E. Newnham'**

This is just one example - searching his name will provide you with other scientific papers, relating to borax, by him.

The lecture delivered by Dr Rex Newnham, where he explained what happened to his Arthritis Cure, was given to the Scottish branch of the McCarrison Society, Dumfries, 5 Oct 2003, Printed in Nutrition and Health.

Ch 6: Ways to use Borax

We decided to devote a whole chapter to the use of Borax, mainly because we have had such good results from using it to control our LS symptoms. *A magnesium supplement is also recommended (see Ch 7)*

If you are still feeling cautious – begin with a bath.

A, Bathing - Standard tub/bath:

a, For your first bath, if you have a standard bath tub, run some HOT water and stir in 1 tablespoon full of borax to dissolve it, then run cool water to a suitable temperature to get into. The bath needs to be deep enough to cover your thighs and reach all the affected areas. Stay in this bath for at least 10 minutes – up to 20, whooshing the water between your legs with your thighs. Do not rinse off, just pat-dry and moisturise any affected parts.
At that level you should have no adverse effects, however, if *even water* stings you there maybe some stinging (obviously) – but most people found it soothing, right from the first dip - as long as they didn't put too much borax in at the start!

b, Happy with that trial? You can try to do this twice a day – or move forward to a full bath to lounge in for at least 20 mins. (if you have the time and the hot water it is very relaxing – not a bad idea considering the effect of stress on LS!)
For a full deep bath add a second tablespoon of borax. Once you are happy that your skin is responding well to borax you can increase the amounts used gradually up to about half a cup - or even more.

Many add other mineral salts too: e.g. bicarbonate of soda, Epsom salts, Himalayan pink salt.
c, Add manipulation: Once you are used to soaking you can add manipulation of the elements of your vulva. This is to help with unfusing if it has happened or to help prevent it. This is just what is suggests, pulling at the labia to loosen any adherence that may be trying to happen, making sure the labia minora are loose and free from the inner of the labia majora, that the clitoral hood is free and mobile. Do this gently and frequently. Sometimes you may find a thin red line appears where they join ... this is usually where some fusing has begun - and you have just freed it. It will sting!
Make sure to moisturise it well and keep it moisturised twice daily so the two sides cannot re-stick easily. (More information on fusing/ absorption in Ch. 10)

B, Sitz bath:
So many of us now do not have a full bath tub, so to soak we have to use something else - and a sitz bath is one option.
These are easily available via the internet - but you need to find one that is suitable for whatever size you are, you need to be able to sit your vulva, perineum and anal area in the borax water, not just perch over it and splash water up. Ask in support groups for recommendations.
a, As with the full bath, dissolve the borax in hot water and add cold to get a suitable temperature to soak in.
b, Start with just one TEASpoonful of borax, and gradually work up to about a tablespoonful.

C, Other tub-ways:
We women are nothing if not inventive. We have seen

all of the following used to soak in borax – grab the idea if it helps you.
A blow-up paddling pool in the base of a shower.
A large-shallow horse-feed bowl, stood in shower.
A plastic under-bed storage box.
A dog bed or a cat-litter tray on top of toilet seat (to act as a sitz-bath).
Just make sure you adjust the amount of borax to use a low amount to begin with and work up to a stronger solution.

To rinse or not to rinse, after a borax soak?
There's no need to rinse after a borax soak, however, if you prefer to, do not rinse your LS affected areas.

NO Tub/Bath

D, Cotton ball method (UK cotton-wool ball method):

Some of us do not have the luxury of having the time to sit in borax water for 10 to 20 minutes twice, or even once, a day.
The cotton-ball method is an on-the-go method – for busy women who have to keep going to get everything done.
Cotton-ball method:
a, Prepare the mixture ahead – it will keep for a long time, use it twice a day if possible.
b, Use a litre jug that can take boiling water:
c, Make a saturated borax solution by starting with boiling water and adding borax little by little until no more borax dissolves. This is called a saturated solution.
d, Store this in a lidded container, and then it can be

left on the counter-top. There may be crystals that form at the bottom. Don't mix in the crystals.
e, Dip cotton(-wool) balls in the solution quickly, and gently squeeze out and tuck the wet cotton balls in the genital area and leave them in place for at least 20 minutes.
f, Don't let the cotton-ball touch the crystals. Do not store cotton-balls in the solution.
g, If you don't like cotton wool try un-fragranced make-up pads - or pieces of clean towelling.

While you 'soak' using this method you can: prepare and eat breakfast, put on your make-up, get the children ready to go, do your hair ... then whip out the cotton(-wool) balls, pat dry, moisturise and go!
Ideas to 'catch drips' from the cotton-balls as you dash around include – reusable cotton panty-liners or period pads, water-proof pants or just a pair of cotton underpants that get borax solution on – and get thrown straight it to the washing machine each time.

E, Squirt bottle / Peri-bottle method:
Sometimes all we can manage is a quick refresh of borax water on our skin – this is when a squirt bottle can help. Also very useful to wash-off urine after urinating.

Squirt-bottle / Peri bottle recipe:
a, Dissolve 1 teaspoon of borax in 1 cup of boiling water, leave to cool.
b, Put in a peri bottle / squirtable bottle and squirt on the genital area after you urinate - or anytime you want, while you are sitting on the toilet.
This washes the urine away from the delicate and sore skin – replacing it with a wash of borax water that

soothes.
Do not wipe-dry with toilet paper, just pat gently to remove drips.

[NB: We acknowledge there are a (very) few people who seem to find borax does not suit them, even at low levels, please see Ch 9 for Other Natural Remedies.
We have also seen that for many of these, it wasn't the borax but something else they were using at the time, and later they re-tried and found borax suited them after all.]

MOISTURISERS

Moisturising recipes enhanced with borax.
As has been said, moisturising is essential after borax soaking. It is dual purpose, it softens and smoothes skin preventing a dry feeling *and* it gives a slip between these delicate skins surfaces, helping to prevent them sticking and causing drag that may lead to a tear or trying to fuse together.

COCONUT OIL BASED:

Ann's Coconut Oil and borax salve – suitable for temperate climes where coconut oil is solid at room temperature: *(for softer crème - see next page)*
Ingredients:
Coconut oil, borax, bicarbonate of soda, lavender essential oil.
Method:
a, Take a tablespoon of coconut oil.
b, Place in a heat-proof MW-safe jug, cover and microwave for about 2 – 3 minutes until hot.
c, Stir in 1 level teaspoon of borax (*ground a bit finer using a pestle and mortar or a grinder) and one level teaspoon of bicarbonate of soda, stir well....

d, Allow to cool a bit, then stir again and again until it thickens. (popping it in the fridge will speed this process – but beware, when it starts to solidify it goes quickly)
e, Add 3 drops of lavender essential oil. Pour into suitable pot, continue stirring until almost set.
f, Chill in fridge initially, to set hard – then store at room temperature.
To use:
g, Scrape a little off the salve – allow it to start melting on your fingers – apply to your vulva, and perineum, especially between labia, rubbing into the joins well. Any gritty bits left you can usually feel with your fingers, wipe these off. Note the last bit in the pot may have more crystals in it – discard and start a new pot. If affected in the anal area apply the salve to that area last.
h, Apply at least morning and evening – plus whenever you feel the need to – like after using the toilet – or when you are about to go out dancing!

***Or** Ann has come up with this modification:*
Coconut Oil and Saturated-Borax-Solution crème Method
A, Make a saturated borax solution: boil the kettle. Put about 2.5 - 3 fluid ounces (75ml) boiling water into a heat-proof mw-safe jug.
B, Teaspoon by teaspoon stir in about 5 - 7 teaspoons of borax powder, until no more dissolves. (You can heat this a bit more in the microwave if it has cooled - to get it to dissolve the maximum amount)
C, In another heatproof jug melt/soften 1 tablespoon of coconut oil.

D, Add 5 teaspoons of the saturated solution to the melted/softened coconut oil.
E, As it begins to cool, whisk with a stick blender.
F, When cool and going opaque - add 3 - 5 drops of lavender oil.
G, Keep returning to whisk the mixture until it begins to thicken - pour into a pot, cover and place in a fridge overnight.
Use as for coconut oil and borax salve above.
Note: this version does not have any gritty bits in it - but is slightly softer. It also has no bi-carb.

Other Coconut Oil ideas:

Add CBD oil to your coconut moisturiser. {CBD = Cannabidiol – comes from the Hemp plant and does not contain the 'high-inducing' THC found in marijuana. CBD is legal in many countries now, but how much of the effective ingredient is in preparations is not always easy to know as it is yet to be regulated for qualities and strengths – as of 2020}

Adding Shea butter and a little castor oil to the coconut oil - and other healing oils such as vitamin E, or tea-tree* (*tea-tree oil can be a bit astringent for some – so test on inner elbow before applying this to your vulva)

WITHOUT Coconut Oil

Though many people have no problem with coconut oil – we are not all the same and some find it itchy or drying.
There are some other solutions people have come up with on the support page over the years to address

the need for 'slip' and moisturising to keep our delicate layers apart – without using Coconut oil.

Here are some other ideas suggested:

A thick oil made by mixing castor oil, borax, and lavender oil. Keep in a small pot and apply daily twice a day, or more as required.

Half and Half extra-virgin olive oil mixed with castor oil. Keep in a small jar and apply as and when required.

A mix of Sesame oil, Olive oil and Jamaican black Castor oil. Keep in a small pot and apply daily twice a day, or more as required.

When to Apply - if you are using Steroid as well:
People's routines vary, but one dermatologist *(on-board with borax soaks)* suggested this routine: borax soak, pat or air-dry, rub in prescribed steroid for 90 seconds, apply moisturiser of choice.

INGESTING BORAX SOLUTIONS:

To achieve their remission, both Allicia and Ann ingested a borax solution, and continue to do so.
As it happens they went about this in different ways – and both worked.

{NOTE: All these protocols call for ingesting a magnesium supplement at half the Recommended Daily Allowance when following the ingestion borax protocol – see Ch 7 for how to choose the best magnesium for you}

1, Maintenance Dose protocol.
This is the way that Allicia went about it – the results are not as fast as the High Dose protocol – taking about 3 – 6 months to see significant results - but many people find this lower-level ingesting preferable.

Method to make a Maintenance Dose (MD)

a, Dissolve 1 rounded **teaspoon** of borax in a litre of boiled water and this becomes your MD concentrate (Maintenance Dose). Keep this in the refrigerator as it will last you quite a while.

b, Drink 2 **teaspoons** of the MD concentrate per day - forever. You can add it to any other drink.

This should give you: 2 teaspoons of solution = 2 x 3mg of boron = 6mg of boron per day.

2, High Dose protocol

This is the route Ann took – and saw significant results within sixteen days. This is a short (14 day) ingesting of a High Dose – followed by Maintenance Dose (at 1-2 teaspoon/s of the maintenance solution) a day thereafter.

Method:
a, Each day – for 14 days – dissolve a **carefully measured 1/8th of a level teaspoon** of borax into a little boiling water. Top up to a litre with cold spring water – drink the whole litre in small amounts over the day.

This gives you 56mg boron per day for the 14 days of the high dose.

b, From the 15th day change to the Maintenance Dose.

Dissolve 1 rounded **teaspoon** of borax in a litre of boiled water and this becomes your **MD** concentrate. Keep this in the refrigerator as it will last you quite a while - and take 1 - 2 **teaspoons** of this per day – forever. This gives a maintenance dose of 3 – 6 mg Boron per day. You can add it to any other drink.

NOTE: This faster, high-dose, method does sometimes result in a **Herxheimer reaction** (sometimes called a toxin-die-off reaction). It is caused by the rapid elimination of toxins and can cause feelings of nausea, or loosening of stools, or headache or, sometimes, you may just feel a bit achy. Even initial aggravation of your symptoms can be experienced. As long as these are mild they will pass in a few days, **if severe, move *immediately* onto the maintenance dose.**

3, Modified High Dose 5:2

a, Dissolve a carefully measured 1/8th of a level teaspoon of borax in a little boiling water - top up to a litre with spring water and drink it in small amounts throughout the day, as for the High Dose protocol.

b, Drink this for 5 days and take 2 days off.

c, Do this for two weeks before going onto a Maintenance Dose. (As described previously)

As with the High Dose protocol – a Herxheimer reaction may be experienced.

Please Note: Do not think - "I'll double the dose for a quicker result"– it doesn't work like that! Stick to the recommended amount.

Also – for those who are interested – excess boron is excreted via urine within 24 hours of ingesting.

Always remember to include a good bio-available magnesium when you are following any borax protocol to enhance the effect of the borax (see Ch.7)

Washing Hair in Borax
- reasons, method and benefits:

You can also wash your hair in Borax - but why would you?
Let's face it - our skin is our largest organ AND it absorbs stuff we put on it. Despite the long-held belief that 'our skin is waterproof, sealing our flesh in and protecting it from *everything*' - IT ISN'T.
Just think 'nicotine patches' - if our skin were truly impermeable these wouldn't work - would they? They don't contain a magic key to open the skin door.

Now, shampoo and conditioners are applied to the whole body if used in either the shower or the bath. Usually they are the last thing to be rinsed - leaving them clinging to your skin.

So, what's wrong with that? Nothing, if you are not concerned about parabens and petrochemicals being left on your skin.
Parabens are there more for the producer than for you - they are a type of preservative. They also happen to be a exonoestrogen and as such are able to mimic oestrogen in the body, and it is this factor that has shown a link to breast cancer.
Petrochemicals? There are some studies out there that say the 1.4 dioxine from these is cancer linked - and others that say the exposure is minimal - that you get more driving your car.
When it comes to all the chemicals that we encounter in the environment many of the dangerous effects are

considered 'minimal' however, when all these 'minimals' in our lives are put together they turn out to be maximal – to have those undesired effects within our body.

So you might want to keep those 'minimal' hazards you can, low or non-existent – so that those you cannot avoid, remain minimal.

There are also lots of other nasties in shampoo and conditioner – some to make the foam, some to then coat the hair after the foaming chemicals have raised all the scales and made it tangly.

Apparently we do not need any of them – our hair and scalp were made to be self-cleaning ... only it takes a while – anything from four weeks to three months to achieve its new equilibrium.

However, this doesn't mean you do not clean your hair – you can go completely cold-turkey on any cleaning product and just wash with warm water – this may take the longest to transition, depending on hair type.

Or you can go the simple solution way, as Ann did – using Bicarbonate of soda and Borax as the 'shampoo' then vinegar (apple-cider) or citric acid as the 'neutraliser/conditioner'.

Borax and Bicarb Hair Washing Method
a, In a large plastic jug (1-2 litres) make up a mixture of 1 dessert-spoon of Borax and 1 dessert-spoon of Bicarbonate of soda [sodium bicarbonate] in about a cup of hot water - top it up to make a litre or more of warm water.

b, Pour it evenly over all your hair - but tip away the last half-inch - which will still have a few un-dissolved gritty bits in it.
c, Massage it in for a minute or two only.
d, Rinse hair thoroughly under the shower.
e, Make up another litre of warm water with 1 teaspoon of citric acid crystals in (you can use a tablespoon of apple-cider vinegar instead, if you prefer).
f, Pour evenly over all your hair.
g, Massage it in a bit - then thoroughly rinse it out.

It sounds long-winded – but really it isn't – as you don't have to work up a lather, and as you are not coating your hair in a thick slime (conditioner) the rinsing takes barely any time at each stage. You only need a large plastic jug to make the mixture up in, and a dessert spoon and a teaspoon, to measure out the ingredients.
Ann claims her hair is so much stronger now - as it does not split or break as it used to - so she can grow it long at last!

ADVANTAGES for LS sufferers.

Instead of leaving your body covered in parabens and petrochemicals – your body has a dousing with borax. Your hair and scalp the same. You will find your hair is clean – and, probably, stays feeling clean longer than it used to.
If you have LP or Psoriasis on your scalp you may find it helps control the symptoms there too.

Ch 7: Magnesium & Other supplements

MAGNESIUM

You will have noticed that each time we have talked about Borax we have recommended taking Magnesium – this is because it **helps to increase the effectiveness of the borax, *even if only bathing in it!***

Magnesium is also vital to human health, especially so for women – and most of us are slightly deficient in this mineral – as we usually get it from food and as soils have become depleted – so our food has become depleted in magnesium.

It helps to balance hormones, and as we know LS is affected by our hormone levels - so do take magnesium. In addition, if you have trouble sleeping – taking your magnesium an hour, to half an hour, before you go to bed will enhance sleep, and, of course, a good night's sleep helps reduce stress – a noted LS flare-trigger.

There are many types of magnesium – and it is important to choose the right one, as some are not very bio-available and so our bodies cannot use the magnesium that is in them. Some are very good, in their own way – but quite expensive and, **as you need to take at least half the Recommended Daily Allowance (RDA) each day** you want a version that won't break the bank.

Then there is the fact that some magnesiums have side effects that you may, or may not, want.

We tend to use one of two versions of magnesium. **Magnesium glycinate**: a good bio-available version of magnesium, without side-effect, that is fairly

inexpensive.
Or **Magnesium citrate:** a good bio-available magnesium with the side-effect of loosening your stools (very useful if you suffer from constipation) and a cheap version of magnesium to buy.

Up to recently it was believed **Magnesium oxide** was not very bio-available. Newer studies have now shown that this is not so, and so it is a suitable supplement to take. It is also inexpensive.
Please, do your own research and make your own choices.

OTHER SUPPLEMENTS & FOODS TO SUPPORT THE SKIN

Apart from Magnesium there are many other supplements that will help support your skin – and as LS affects the skin you may find some, or all, of these useful to you.
We have started the list with those that we find useful and use on a daily basis – followed by other recommendations from the 'collected wisdom' of other sufferers from LS (and in some cases LP)

Vitamin D3:
The sunshine vitamin – this vitamin we manufacture in our own skin under certain conditions* and **is essential to overall health and to the health of our skin, bones and our immune system.**
*(that good levels of UVB light falls on significant areas of our exposed skin. This means that in Britain or northern states in the USA, for instance, because of the northerly latitude, the UVB sun rays are only strong enough to create vitamin D in our skin from

May to October, and then, generally between 10am and 2pm, the 20 mins across noon being optimum.) Vitamin D is also only available from a limited range of foods – including cod liver oil, swordfish, salmon, canned tuna, beef liver, egg yolks and sardines. That said, you would need to eat them nearly every day to get enough vitamin D - the best one being cod-liver oil, which you may be taking for other reasons anyway.

You might like to consider taking a Vitamin D3 supplement just to be sure, especially in winter.

Zinc:
The skin is the third most zinc abundant tissue in the body, and having sufficient zinc helps wound healing – a useful addition when our LS skin is so often damaged.
Zinc is naturally found in many foods, but meats, seafood, dairy products, nuts, legumes, and whole grains offer relatively high levels of zinc.

You often find Zinc supplements in association with Vitamin C - it is worth having both.

Vitamin C:
The provision of Vitamin C to the skin greatly assists wound healing and minimises raised scar formation. This has been demonstrated in numerous clinical studies in humans and animals. Skin fibroblasts have an absolute dependence on vitamin C for the synthesis of collagen, and for the regulation of the collagen/elastin balance in the dermis. So you can see why it would be useful to maintain good levels of Vitamin C when suffering from LS.
Good skin health is positively associated with fruit and

vegetable intake in a number of well-executed intervention studies.
Vitamin C is found in fruits and veg such as oranges and orange juice, red and green peppers, strawberries, blackcurrants, broccoli, brussel-sprouts and potatoes. Vitamin C isn't stored in the body – so daily intake is recommended.

Vitamin K1:
Known as the blood-clotting vitamin.
Generally if you eat sufficient green leafy vegetables you will have enough vitamin K1 in your diet.

Vitamin K2:
A little known vitamin, but required for the process that supports calcium deposit into bones.

Dietary K2 is found in egg yolk, liver, cheeses and certain fermented vegetables (synthesised by the fermenting bacteria)

Vitamin A:
Both the upper and lower layers of skin need vitamin A. It helps the oil glands around your hair follicles work and may also help cuts and scrapes heal, especially if you're taking steroids to reduce inflammation. It seems to prevent sun damage by interrupting the process that breaks down collagen.
Vitamin A is found in eggs and leafy dark greens – so easy to incorporate into your diet.

Vitamin B2:
There is evidence that B vitamins - particularly **B2** support healthy skin cell growth. B2 can be found in milk, plain yoghurt, eggs & mushrooms.

Vitamin E:
Vitamin E is both an antioxidant and anti-inflammatory and can also absorb the energy from UV light, which damages skin and leads to wrinkles, sagging, and skin cancer. It is also important as it works with vitamin C to strengthen cell walls - and when we suffer from thinning skin with LS this is important.
Vitamin E is also found in eggs and green leafy veg as well as avocados and extra virgin olive oil.

Selenium:
Selenium is a mineral that helps certain antioxidants protect your skin from UV rays. However, in our case, selenium deficiency has been linked with a greater chance of skin cancer, and with LS giving a raised chance it is wise to make sure Selenium is working on our side.
The richest food sources of Selenium are found in Brazil nuts, seafoods, and organ meats - other sources include muscle meats, flax-seeds, spinach, cereals and other grains, and dairy products.

Boron:
This is why we take borax. You can take boron drops - but apparently it is even more effective if you go for the 'cheap' option of borax solution (as carefully described in the protocols). Boron is also found in fruits and vegetables but it depends a lot on the quantity of boron in the soil - and many farmed soils are depleted in boron. High boron foods include avocados, apples, pears, peanuts, beans, grapes, oranges.

Collagen:

Collagen is responsible for the elasticity in our skin. There is some evidence that suggests that taking collagen supplements, which are essentially the collagen proteins broken down into their peptides, does help with this. It is often taken together with Hyaluronic acid - and there is some emerging evidence that this combination works too.

The best food that contains collagen is bone-broth - made by boiling down animal bones in liquid - and if you go Paleo, you will find plenty of information about this. However, this does not break it down to peptides - only as far as gelatine - for which there is not the evidence that it is broken down further in digestion to make the peptides available.

Bone broth has other immune strengthening properties however, so is a good bet, and can be supplemented with powdered collagen peptide - or these can be taken on their own.

Hyaluronic acid:

Hyaluronic acid is a major component of skin and is involved in wound repair - so we can see why it would be helpful in a condition where the skin needs repairing often.

There is some evidence that says hyaluronic acid supplements, at the 100-200mg range of supplementation, is effective. (though it was the effect on knee joints that was measured)

As for foods to eat to raise your levels of hyaluronic acid naturally, bone-broth is a good one, as is liver, soy foods, sweet potatoes, citrus fruits, dark-green leafy vegetables, dark red fruit & vegetables, flax seeds and walnuts.

Then there are the foods we eat
and what we need from them

Healthy Fats:
This is how your skin gets its 'glow.' Too little fat in your diet can make your skin wrinkled and dry.
Omega-3 and Omega-6 essential fatty acids, which your body can't make but needs to build cell walls, are found in types of polyunsaturated fat. They are also important for brain function as the myelin sheath, that surrounds the nerves that send messages in the brain, is made with these and Omega-9 fatty acids.
They also block a chemical that lets skin cancer grow and spread, and they help to inhibit inflammation.

Focus on Omega-3 essential fatty acids from plants, like flax seed, or oily fish, like salmon, mackerel or sardines. Omega-3 helps your skin function properly and stay moist, firm, and flexible.
Though Omega-6 fatty acids are also essential - try not to consume too much made with, or fried in, polyunsaturated oils with high levels of Omega-6, such as those from corn or sunflower seeds - as consuming these can prevent the uptake of the more essential Omega-3s. The ideal ratio is four or less Omega-6 to each Omega-3 consumed.
Virgin Olive oil is a 73% mono-unsaturated oil made of **oleic fatty acids (Omega-9)**, also good for the skin, reducing inflammation and building the myelin sheath.
You may be surprised to find that Lard is 42% **oleic fatty acids** and 11% polyunsaturated fats.

Protein:
Your body turns the proteins you eat into building

blocks called amino acids and reuses them to make other proteins, including the collagen and keratin that form the structure of skin. Amino acids also help slough off old skin.
Some amino acids are antioxidants that protect skin cells against UV rays and from 'free radicals' made when your body breaks down certain foods or is around cigarette smoke.

Foods and Supplements:
In general, **fruits and vegetables are good choices** because they have skin-friendly vitamins and other antioxidants.

Some foods offer more than one nutrient for your skin, which often helps them work better:
Fatty fish: (salmon, sardines, tuna): protein, omega-3s, selenium.
Leafy dark greens: (kale, spinach, collards): vitamins A, C, and E; omega-3s; protein - plus selenium in spinach.
Eggs: protein, vitamins A and E, selenium, zinc.
Flaxseeds: omega-3s, selenium.
Legumes: (lentils, chickpeas): protein, zinc.
Avocados: healthy fats, vitamins C and E.
Extra virgin olive oil: oleic acid fats, vitamin E.

Talk to your doctor if you're concerned you're not getting enough of these key nutrients from your food to make sure supplements won't affect your health in other ways. Fish oil is a source of omega-3s, for example, but taking it may not be a good idea if you're on blood thinners or have a weakened immune system. And zinc supplements can make some antibiotics less effective.

Ch 8: Borax / Steroid / or Both? And what about vulval cancer?

One of the biggest questions we see asked is whether to use steroids ... or not.

We have no problem with anyone choosing to use the steroid option. It may work perfectly for you and, with an understanding doctor who will optimise the potency of the prescribed steroid, it may work for you in the long term without causing any side effects.

You already know we have no problem with the borax route – but neither do we have a problem with anyone mixing and matching as suits their own body.

The aim is to keep the inflammation down, the irritation away and the skin looking a healthy normal colour, intact and not sticking together or swollen.

We have a little bit of a problem with those who insist to others that steroid use is the only option – taking no account that for some people it is not an option. The steroid use may cause serious side-effects, it may cause burning or a rash, it may be in-effective at reducing the symptoms or may have become so after a time.

We also have a problem with those people who tell you point blank that steroid use is the **only** way to guarantee you will not get vulval cancer. This is scary and unhelpful to people for whom the steroid is not a useful solution to their LS misery.

This assertion is usually based on a study carried out in Australia (To look for the published paper: s**earch** for: *Long-term Management of Adult Vulvar Lichen Sclerosus A Prospective Cohort Study of 507 Women Andrew Lee, MBBS; Jennifer Bradford, MBBS; Gayle Fischer, MD.*) They carried out a study that used **individually tailored potencies of steroid cream and frequent follow-ups over seven years.** They report that vulval cancer did not appear in any of the 'fully compliant' women, yet it did in 4.7% of the 'partially-compliant'. In their study, out of the 357 compliant patients, none developed carcinoma during the follow-up years. However, of the 150 partly compliant patients, 7 did show signs of a carcinoma in the same time. This put their risk of cancer at 4.7% - which is close to the 5 – 6% risk found in untreated women in previous studies. They went on to say that this suggests that just using a treatment when it felt like it needed it (for instance just to control the symptoms when they flared) did not reduce the risk of cancer. They added that this supported the findings in previous studies that suggested that full compliance with treatment could, potentially, reduce the incidence of cancer. Concluding: "It seems that, in compliant patients **who maintain normal skin color and texture**, the risk of VSN (*vulval squamous neoplasm*) is greatly reduced." *(Quotes from the Abstract)*

In the full paper we are not told anything else about the partially-compliant women. We do not know if they found the steroids hurt them, or didn't seem to work, or stopped working or they had other issues in their life (stress forming perhaps?) that made them less compliant. We would have thought that if the steroids offered were the answer to their misery - they would have been compliant.

From Cancer Research UK we have this quote:
"Lichen Sclerosus and lichen planus cause long term (chronic) **irritation of the skin of the vulva.** This may be a possible **cause of the increased cancer risk.**"

It is quite possible that it is the constant damage and repair of the delicate skin of the vulva, (as in the scratch-itch cycle) when the symptoms are not relieved that gives cancer the opportunity to develop – as repeated injury and repair to our bodies mean more reproduction of cells than normal – and each time a cell reproduces there is the chance of a mutation.

Inflammation also appears to have a dual role in this. **Search** in PMC for *"Tumor Promotion via Injury - and death-induced Inflammation' by Ali Kuraishy, Michael Karin, and Sergei I. Grivennikov"*
For this study they set out to answer the question of whether the prevalence of inflammation could be the link between tissue injury and cancer – as recent studies had made clear the particular importance of of inflammation in both processes. These showed that inflammation doesn't just protect injured tissues from infection nor just cause the removal of damaged cells – but instead is critical to nearly every stage of tissue repair and tumorgenisis.
Their theory was that injury causes inflammation, which then co-ordinates and instigates wound healing and tissue regeneration. However, if the cause of the inflammation is not resolved or is "**chronically**

provoked by repetitive injury or other factors, the resulting unchecked wound healing process can promote cancer formation". This assertion is supported by a large body of data. (Which can be found in the full paper)
"These conclusions also suggest the therapeutic approaches that minimise injury and restore normal tissue homeostasis can be used in cancer prevention." *(Quotes from the Abstract)*

In other words, stopping the damage and the inflammation - in whatever way - can be useful in cancer prevention.

Before we get too focused on the cancer aspect - we still have to remember that vulval cancer is rare - even for women who have LS - a factor that makes it slightly more likely.

Conclusion: It is your choice whether to use the steroid route, borax route - or both, to suppress the symptoms, particularly any that cause damage to the skin or inflammation. However, keeping both damage and inflammation down seems to be key in protecting yourself from increased possibility of developing vulval cancer.
One thing is certain from the literature on vulval cancer – if you have LS, no matter how you are treating it to keep the symptoms down, you ought to make sure someone, who knows what vulval cancer looks like, looks at your vulva at least once a year, be it a sexual health nurse, a gynaecologist or a dermatologist. Also, seek their advice if you notice anything different happening in your vulval region - lumps, bumps or discoloured spots. Recognition and early treatment are very important for good outcomes.

Ch 9: Other Natural Remedies - collated wisdom

1, Along with their borax baths, **or instead of Borax baths - for those who find it doesn't suit them,** some people use other/extra ingredients:

Some people use/add baking soda (bicarbonate of soda), others use/add Himalayan pink salt, and others use/add Epsom salts (magnesium sulphate).

2, **Apple Cider Vinegar** (make sure you use organic and make sure it says 'with the mother' – as otherwise it will be processed and will not work as well)

Apply ACV diluted 50/50 with water to the vulva. If this stings, you can make the solution up with more water.

With this method it is essential that you also take ACV internally too, a tablespoon taken twice a day in a glass of warm spring water. Some people also add half a teaspoon of baking soda to this mix.

3, **Lavender oil** is also effective when included in ingredients used on LS skin (such as a few drops in a coconut oil balm). However it can be applied directly and will stop the itch in a short time. Use a good quality essential oil for either application.

4, **Castor Oil** can be used on LS skin.
To make a balm use 4 tablespoons of castor oil, mix in 2 – 3 drops of lavender essential oil and 1-2 drops of lemon-grass essential oil and put in a jar. This mixture will make a sort-of paste that sticks to the skin and gives relief from the itch, as well as helping sore spots

heal. It can be a little messy leaving marks on underwear – but a cloth liner (like a folded cotton handkerchief) will help prevent problems.

5, **Honey,** particularly on those fine cuts and abrasions – has been used by some people effectively to ease and help the healing. Use organic if possible.

6, **Colloidal Silver,** also used for healing the fine cuts.

7, **Homeopathy** works for some people, but to get real benefit you need individual consultations.

8, **Change your diet.** There are ways of eating that have helped many people lessen the effect of their LS symptoms. Information on these is given in Ch 11 (Flares and Triggers) and it would seem that a change of diet to avoid triggers is wise, and some ways of eating will not only help avoid triggers but also boost your body's resistance to infections.

Many women with LS also report having candida issues – so an anti-candida diet might be considered to remove that distraction and isolate the LS to be focused on.

The Anti-candida diet cuts out all refined sugars and carbohydrates, all yeast containing foods, all artificial sweeteners, sweetened or highly processed dairy, wheat and other gluten grains, but then includes probiotics (like fermented foods) and prebiotics (food that supports beneficial bacteria).

Some people use all, or a selection, of these together, everyone of us is different - experiment and see what suits your body and controls your LS best.

Ch 10: Fusing/Absorption/Agglutination/ Atrophy/Adhesion/Scarring/Bruising

Sadly, many of us hear nothing about these aspects of LS from our doctors - it is only after we joined a support group or started researching on the internet or, suddenly realised in horror, that we had changed in appearance 'down there' that we come across these terms - and the pictures that illustrate them in all their extreme conditions.

This is all very scary - we realise, and have experienced some of it ourselves. The good news is that, despite what the doctors say, *some* of this is reversible if caught early enough - and some preventable if we know what is likely to happen and how to try to prevent it.

What is meant by these terms?
To begin with - even some doctors seem to mix and match some of the terms.
Fusing (agglutination/adhesion) *with* **Absorption/ Atrophy** - in particular. We have seen these described in identical ways - as if they are interchangeable. They aren't.
Atrophy presents as thinning, wasting away, of labia in particular, completed by shrinking back into the main tissues (**Absorption**) this probably *is* irreversible.

However, ***fusing is more common*** and ***may look like*** absorption, even to doctors used to looking at LS.

Fusing: What is clear is that the labia may fuse - that is stick together (they sometime use the term ***agglutinate*** - which means to 'cause to ***adhere***: fasten')

These may fuse in a variety of ways:
The labia minora may fuse to each other, sealing off the interior of the vulva, the urethra and the clitoral hood, down to and including covering the entrance to the vagina. This type of fusing can cause many problems, including retention of urine so that it dribbles out long after urination has taken place, and retention and subsequent dribbling out of the menses (menstrual blood) in menstruating women. This extreme 'loss of architecture' does seem to require surgery, particularly to open up the vagina again, however, for the rest there is some hope for un-fusing without surgery, especially if caught early.
The clitoral hood may fuse in itself, preventing retraction and 'burying the clitoris' so reducing sensation.
The labia minora, may fuse to the inside of the labia majora – and therefore ***seem*** to disappear altogether.

The latter two fusings appear to be the type of fusing that can be easiest reversed, by home-treatment of various kinds.

If we know from the outset that fusing is a likelihood then it is possible that a combination of 'home methods' may prevent the skin of the labia becoming 'sticky' and adhering to each other. *As it stands most people are not told what to expect anyway - so they have no chance to try to prevent it.*

What can be done to reverse Fusing?

Borax soaking and manipulation: from reports on support groups this method has seen many people loosen stuck-down or stuck together (fused) labia minora or clitoral hoods.

Reports of successfully using estrogen/oestrogen creams and manipulation, have also been received.

It can be a little painful either way – as the newly released skin is highly sensitive and delicate.
With both treatments it is not a fast process – and may not be a complete process.
As soon as any un-fusing is achieved it is essential that the skin of the labia must always be well moisturised, at least twice daily with something that prevents them adhering again in the future. This is an ongoing treatment.

Manipulation - how to:
Whether soaking in borax in the bath, or after using the cotton-ball method to soak, or after applying oestrogen creams, if you can manually pull the labia around and ease the layers apart then this can help with un-fusing. Do not be too rough, but it will hurt a bit if it begins to un-fuse.
Make sure that you moisturise with something that will keep the layers apart afterwards – like coconut oil salve – or whatever suits your body.

Q-tip (cotton-bud) method – helping to un-fuse labia minora and clitoral hood:

This is a method to try daily, or even twice daily, maybe after your borax-soaks.
Make the same saturated borax solution as the solution for the cotton ball method (as described in Ch:6) and then dip the Q-tip (cotton-bud) in the solution and use the wet Q-tip to treat very specific spots by gently rubbing the Q-tip all over the fused spots.
You can even find openings in your fused areas to

insert the tip of the q-tip into, and to twist it gently round and round, particularly if the inner labia have fused to each other over the vulva, or the clitoral hood is fused and immobile. This may help to separate the skin and un-fuse.

If you are not keen on borax or wish to use something else this can be done using estrace, softened coconut oil, or your steroid cream - if you are finding it works for you.

You may need to sit facing a mirror, or over a mirror, to see what you are doing. You may need to pull the labia or clitoral hood to spot any gaps in the fusing and, once located, release them to try to insert the tip of the cotton-bud (Q-tip) into the gap.

Do not worry if only the tiniest end can get in the gap – each time it will be a little easier. Always make sure the Q-tip is moisturised or wet so that it doesn't pull on the delicate skin.

It may also be sore just after working on it – this is usually because there has been a little separating of the skin surfaces and they will feel raw. Make sure you moisturise well to help prevent them re-sticking.

Do not give up, but be gentle with yourself, this process can take daily treatments for months to work fully.

Once un-fused, maintain the moisturising – and occasionally run through the Q-tip method again to be sure.

[Note: pointed-end Precision Q-tips (cotton-buds UK) are now available – these may be better to use - certainly to begin with]

[We understand that the late Dee Troll was probably the first person to suggest this method, and so acknowledge her contribution here]

Scarring – and avoidance of:
Though fusing can be reversed – this is not so for scarring once it has occurred. Damage that could form a scar can be moisturised, stretched and massaged so that it doesn't form such a hard or tight scar, but once it is there it is very difficult to do much to alleviate the problem of the extra tightness and the tendency to split rather than stretch.
The primary aim, therefore, is to prevent the scratching that results in most of the damage. As described previously – calming the itch is the main way to achieve this – whether by borax bathing (of one sort or the other) borax ingestion, other natural methods or by steroid use.

Scarring also occurs from splitting the skin – which sometimes can occur during sex, but even through general exercise if your skin is thin and tight. The healing can then cause more scarring which reduces the stretchiness and can then lead to more skin damage.
To alleviate this doctors will often prescribe a topical oestrogen pessary (if you are in menopause), vaginal dilators and a lubricant for use during sex.
(more details of lubricants and ways to gently stretch the scar- tightened skin in Chapter 12)

Bruising:
Many people mention bruising, with the usual attendant colours, or sometimes 'blood blisters'. With LS the whole area is more tender than usual - and can bruise easily. Being aware of your vulva and how it looks normally can help you decide if the discolouration is just bruising or something else.

Ch 11: Flares, Triggers and how to manage them.

FLARES: what do we mean by a Flare?

You will hear people who say they are going through a 'flare' - it is what it sounds like – a flare-up in their condition. Suddenly they are in extra pain, have extra swelling or itching, suddenly it is unbearable and they do not always know why.

Through listening to the group some 'culprits' have emerged. However, as everyone's body is different you will have to try out different things to find *your* triggers. A good way to do this is to cut out the lot – then, when the flare has subsided, re-introduce one at a time (one a week say) watching for any signs of a new flare beginning.

This is a huge area and we can only touch on the most common aspects here.

TRIGGERS and ways to manage them

FOOD:
There appears to be a significant link between what you eat and flares.
The main things that people have found it helps to cut out of their diet have been:

Gluten:
This is a well-known inflammatory – and if your gut health has been compromised at any time (gut-biome disrupted by medication, like antibiotics, or by food choices that do not support beneficial gut bacteria) it

could be a factor, especially as the gliadin in gluten helps create a leaky-gut, allowing it and other inflammatory molecules into your system.

Added sugars:
Sugar (sucrose, glucose, fructose - especially High Fructose Corn Syrup) is also an inflammatory and, as with Gluten, can be an active irritant with disrupted gut-biome issues. It is also to be remembered that carbohydrates are, in general, just one digestive process away from being sugars.

Alcohol:
Alcohol is also an inflammatory, and more, it helps allow Lipopolysaccharide (LPS) enter the blood, and thereby the body system, and LPS has been shown to be a major inflammatory substance.
Don't forget that beers also contain gluten.

Oxalate:
For some people - Oxalate in foods is a problem.
These foods can be avoided or reduced in the diet, if you find they cause your LS to flare.
High-oxalate fruits include: berries, kiwis, figs, purple grapes.
Vegetables that contain high levels of oxalate include: rhubarb, okra, leeks, spinach, beets, Swiss chard.
Seeds and legumes to avoid include: almonds, cashews, peanuts, soy products.
Some grain products are also high in oxalate, including: bran flakes, wheat germ, quinoa.
The following foods are also high in oxalate: cocoa, chocolate, tea.

Nightshades: Food from the 'nightshade family' affect

some people causing flares. These include tomatoes, potatoes, peppers & eggplants (aubergines).

Corn/maize:
Some people have reported that Corn (Maize) in its many guises has shown to be their trigger for a flare. As an ingredient Corn can be as cornflour, used as a thickening agent in many pre-made products, corn syrup, HFCS (High Fructose Corn Syrup) used to sweeten many products including drinks, and in everything maize related from corn-flakes to tacos.

Milk products:
For some people milk products can cause inflammatory reactions. We would suggest any milk products consumed, wherever possible, should come from milk producers that do not depend on antibiotics (non-therapeutic) or hormones (rBST, rBGH) for high milk yields, and from mostly pastured animals, rather than 'industrialised' (common in USA) farming.
If the milk products still cause problems – then maybe you are lactose intolerant – this may depend upon your heritage.
Though about 65% of the total human population has a reduced ability to digest lactose after infancy, lactose intolerance in adulthood is most common in people of East Asian descent, with over 70% of them affected. Lactose intolerance is also very common in people of West African, Arab, Jewish, Greek, and Italian descent.
However, the prevalence of lactose intolerance is very low in populations with a long history of dependence on unfermented milk products as an important food source. So only about 5% of people of Northern European descent are lactose intolerant.

TYPES of DIET to help manage Food triggers:

AIP (Auto-Immune Protocol)
The AIP is an elimination diet, it involves not eating certain types of food for several weeks at a time and carefully noting any effects on health upon re-introduction.
This is what you might try to identify any food triggers you may have.
The diet is very similar to the Paleo (see below) - but excludes nightshades (such as tomatoes, potatoes, peppers and eggplants) grains, legumes, dairy, some vegetable oils, coffee, nuts and seeds, alcohol and food additives, such as refined or added sugars.

Paleo:
This 'way of life diet' avoids grains (of all kinds) and beans (the seeds of the bean rather than the green-flesh) legumes, root crops, fruits (except some berries) and all ready-made products including anything with artificial sweeteners. Paleo also has an emphasis on eating pasture-fed organic meats only and, if taken, dairy – as well as a range of 'above-ground' organic vegetables. It meets many of the criteria for avoiding many of the triggers for flares.

Keto: is very similar to the Paleo – except the aim is to keep carb intakes below 5% of total energy (again – this avoids eating many of the flare-triggers).

Carnivore: A more extreme version of Paleo – it is a high fat, high protein diet that has no plant content – and so also avoids the oxalates still present in the Paleo or Keto diets.

IF – Intermittent Fasting:

Intermittent Fasting means that you abstain from food and all drink (except water, black tea or coffee) for a period of time - usually in excess of 18 hours, but generally less than 48 - once or twice a week. This seems to have an affect on lessening symptoms - maybe to do with avoidance of triggers, or maybe to do with the gut-biome. It is uncertain – but many find it makes them feel better in many ways – so it is worth mentioning here and maybe trying for yourself.

[Do research IF yourself – there are many variants and time-scales]

LOW-Oxalate diet:

Cutting out high-oxalate foods can helps some people. See previous section on **Oxalates as triggers** for more information on high-oxalate foods.

SUPPORTING your gut-biome.

As said LS, and other auto-immune conditions, are frequently linked to dysbiosis (disrupted gut-microbiome) or leaky gut. One way to help alleviate LS therefore would be to enhance your gut-biome. The following are foods that add beneficial gut bacteria.

Fermented Foods and Drinks:

Not really a diet – but a good way to support your good gut bacteria, that then help prevent leaky-gut.

Pickles: *{NOTE- these **do not** contain vinegar}*

Sauerkraut, Kimchi, fermented pickled onions, fermented carrots all can be made easily at home. Recipes are easily available on the internet – start with the simple ones and always be scrupulously hygienic in making them.

Incidentally for oxalate sensitive people, *research shows that fermenting high oxalate vegetables decreases the amount of oxalate in the vegetable. *(search: 'effect of fermentation on silverbeet oxalate' to find a science paper on NCBI)*

[Note 1: Canned or jar versions bought from un-chilled supermarket shelves will not have any live bacteria in them – as they have to sterilise them before sealing tight]

[Note 2: one person in the support group has said that fermented foods triggered their flare]

Yoghurt/yogurt:

Yoghurt is a fermented food – and is well known for supporting the gut biome – as long as it is LIVE and, preferably, unsweetened (we do not want to have added sugars or artificial sweeteners).

Buy organic live yoghurt or make your own!

[Ann uses an electronic pressure cooker, which has a yoghurt making setting, to make about 6 pints at a time – but any yoghurt making method will do – you can use a small bought live yoghurt as a starter but remember to be scrupulous in cleanliness when you make and jar your yoghurt for keeping in the fridge]

Cheeses:

Quality cheeses are also a fermented product. Try to buy block cheeses, or soft cheeses, made from organic or pastured-fed cows and, if you can get it at all, made

from raw-milk.
Avoid the highly processed cheeses (the ones generally used for pre-cut slices, spreadables, strings etc) as the heat-treatments these go through probably destroy any beneficial bacteria.

Kefir: Milk kefir - Water kefir

Milk kefir is a fermented milk product that supports the good gut bacteria, with a sour acquired taste. Buy a starter online, and follow the simple instructions to make it.
A water-kefir version is available for people who do not like milk or prefer a less sour version - this is made with sweetened fruit-water - nearly all the sugar being used by the Kefir organism, and leaving a refreshing effervescent drinks packed with lots of beneficial probiotics to support your gut biome - a good substitute for fizzy soda drinks.
Both starter grains are available online - and there are plenty of guides to getting started, however, as the grains grow and multiply it might be worth asking friends if they make it and if they have some grains going spare.

Kombucha:

Very similar to water kefir - except, instead of grains the organism makes a thick gelatinous pad that floats on top of the sweetened tea it feeds on, leaving an effervescent liquid full of probiotics for you to drink. Like kefir grains the Kombucha mother reproduces so ask if anyone has one to pass on before looking to buy online. Again, plenty of sites to explain the methods.

NOTE: Also research the foods that support and feed the beneficial bacteria in your gut-biome - and include them in your dietary choices.
If you have taken a long-course of antibiotics, or similar, that may have wiped out your gut bacteria, consider a good quality multi-strain bacteria probiotic as a gut-biome 'starter'.

PHARMACEUTICAL TRIGGERS:

This is a huge area again, but as people with LS use a lot of creams/ointments/moisturisers, and these can contain ingredients that trigger a flare in *some* people, we have concentrated on these, using information from 'collated wisdom'.

Petroleum based products seem to be a problem for many - though not all.
The best known of these is Vaseline – which is often recommended by doctors as a barrier, and is useful in that and is cheap. It seals off the surface, almost completely, so not allowing your skin to breathe at all, but also sealing in any fungi or bacteria that were on your skin before application. It is also 'heavy' and feels greasy – many ladies swear by it, but for us, the idea that it is a good thing to put a petroleum by-product on your most delicate skin is difficult to accept. By the way – if you find it does not agree with you and want to avoid it, you will find it in so many products – sometimes called 'mineral oil' or

‘petrolatum’ as it is a very cheap ingredient and used for a variety of properties.

Emu oil-based products:
For some, these are the answer to a prayer. For others it can cause a reaction and a flare. Try a small amount first - as it is expensive to have standing on a shelf - they sometimes offer a small sample to try.

Lanolin-based products:
Though a natural product, from the fleece of sheep, lanolin can also trigger flares in people who find wool an irritant. It works better than vaseline, as it does not stop the skin breathing. However, it also seems to be combined with petrolatum to make many products – read the ingredients.

Coconut oil-based products:
These *do not seem to trigger flares as such* – but *some* people have said they find the coconut oil ‘drying’. Cheap and easy to try out for yourself.

Managing pharmaceutical triggers *depends on understanding exactly what it is in the preparation that triggers the flare. Only you, by being conscious of what you are putting on, or in, your body, can identify the trigger.*
Be aware of the ‘extra’ ingredients in all ‘medications’, ***including steroid creams or ointments****, even the ‘carriers’ within some tablets or the cases of some capsules.* ***Your*** *notes and research will be your guide as to which pharmaceutical items are* ***your*** *triggers and what to avoid.*

CYCLIC BODY TRIGGERS:

There is strong evidence that LS is linked to our oestrogen levels. So it is not surprising that for many LS sufferers, who are not children or who are not in menopause, the natural monthly hormone cycle will trigger flares – for some it is before their period, for some during, and for others after.

Managing cyclic body triggers: There seems to be little we can do to change this unless on medication that flattens the variation, such as is used for birth-control - however, for some, this may prove to present other triggers.

PSYCHOLOGICAL TRIGGERS:

STRESS flares:

A 'hidden' but significant culprit for triggering a flare appears to be STRESS. For sure – when you have a flare you are often stressed by that – but it is frequently possible to spot the stress occurring before the flare hit.

First you need to be aware when stress is getting to the point where it might trigger a flare – then you need to have some ways to defuse the stress.

Just to be clear – there are different types of stress. **Good stress** tends to be stress that motivates us, usually associated with something we want to achieve and is achievable, and over which we have control. This is short-term and usually results in a great feeling of accomplishment when we use the energy to gain our goal.

Bad stress is different. It is often imposed from above, external, put upon us, with expectations that feel unachievable, or from circumstances over which we have no control. Often, even achieving the perceived goal only results in finding there is another layer to work through, or another bigger problem.

When we have become so accustomed to our daily (externally placed) stress, that sometimes we don't even notice that we feel like this all the time, it is called **Chronic Stress** – and is bad for us in so many ways – and can lead to flares.

To manage these psychological triggers - look for ways to modify and avoid stress:

Soaking in a bath is a wonderful way to relieve stress - and also alleviate Lichen Sclerosus symptoms when you add your borax.

Set aside time daily for journaling. It is a great way to unplug from your everyday stresses and can give you a sense of direction.

Set goals that are realistic and set aside time for yourself.

Meditation, yoga, or prayer is a great way to quiet the mind.

Get plenty of exercise and plenty of sleep. Try to get outside in the fresh air for at least an hour, daily, preferably in the early morning.

Focus on positive thoughts. List things you can be grateful for.

Start the day saying, out loud, five things you are grateful for, end the day in the same way.

Spend time with your pet or listening to music.

Try massages, aromatherapy, shiatsu or acupuncture.

And try not to focus too much on the LS itself - it is not who you are - once you can manage the symptoms, the stress about it will ease.

Ch 12: Sex Life / Pregnancy

Even though this condition can hit us at almost any age, sex isn't paid much attention to, but - as the *classic patient* is a menopausal woman ... and the *classic doctor* is a man – we are not surprised.

However, whatever age, sex is an important part of how we feel and how we think of ourselves. Therefore it is important that, suffering from a condition that attacks us at the heart of our sexuality, this is addressed.
People write that they feel 'less of a woman' when their structure disappears, less of a woman, when the pain prevents intercourse, less sexy altogether knowing what is going on down there ... and none of this is our fault, yet it is almost ignored by the medical fraternity.

Talk to your partner:

Things that are a 'must know':
It is not a sexual transmitted disease.
It is not 'catching' (contagious).
It won't 'go away' in a week or two ... it is for life.
The skin becomes thin and fragile.
That there are examples of people who have found things that take away the pain and itching.
That there are things that can help – but it is a case of finding what works for you - both.

With regard to making love:
Patience is required.
Good lubrication is required.

[Your own research is required to make sure the chosen lubricants do not irritate your LS skin – the product 'Yes' is said by some to be good in this way, as is the silicone 'Lube-life', and 'Aloe-cadabra' lube, or the product 'Julva'. Others suggest sesame oil, almond oil, coconut oil, jojoba oil or Vitamin E oil as natural lubes.
Please be aware that some lubricants can make condoms ineffective! Be wary of those containing Glycerine (as this can encourage Thrush) or are 'thick' like KY jelly (as this draws moisture from the tissues of the vagina) or contain parabens (as they are endocrine disrupters in the body.)]

Maybe changes of position will help.
Maybe help with using dilators to help stretch / re-elasticise the skin around the entrance to the vagina if tight and liable to split. The Milli has been mentioned as it is silicone and adjustable.
Maybe abstention, if too painful or too much damage is caused by penetration.
In which case there are 'other ways' to achieve closeness and sexual release – and that these can be researched and engaged in - such as Tantric sex, Slow sex, or look for the TED talk by Diane Richardson about Mindful sex.
Many also recommend a borax bath/peri-bottle rinse after sex helps too, especially if your partner's sperm seems to irritate your LS skin - as it does some.

Some partners do not want to 'look' at all - others are involved in the 'treatment' helping to massage in creams, or looking to note, or photograph for their women to see changes in architecture. Whatever is best in your relationship and is best for you is ok. We are all different.

Pregnancy:

Though neither of us has been through a pregnancy while suffering from LS – there are plenty of women in the group who have been, or are, pregnant while having LS – so this section is all 'collated wisdom'.

To begin with, the changes in the hormones during pregnancy can change the way that the LS manifests itself.
For some it is a blessing, in that the LS may ease up, go into remission, and seem to disappear during the actual pregnancy.
Some find it is a mixture of flares and no-flare – again, probably driven by the variation in hormone levels as the pregnancy progresses.
For some, pregnancy *seems* to be the trigger for the LS to appear – or at least be recognised – this mainly with asymptomatic cases (Cases where the LS causes white plaques but, at that point, none of the distressing itching, splitting, swelling or soreness that most feel). This makes sense to a certain degree – as most of us, unfortunately, do not examine our vulvas unless we feel something wrong 'down there', so these women would not have gone to a doctor or gynaecologist with a problem in the area - so the condition had not been spotted by someone who knows what they are looking at until the ante-natal examinations.

Vaginal delivery:
There is a lot of concern about delivering vaginally when suffering from LS – due to the delicacy of the skin.

This is a matter to discuss with your gynaecologist - and birth-team - as each woman is different and her experience of LS is different.
However, from the collated wisdom, many deliver vaginally without more skin distress than in women not suffering from LS. This may be because, as long as the vagina entrance has not been scarred and compromised, it is the vagina that has to do all the stretching (not the vulva) and LS does not affect the interior of the vagina. (NB Lichen Planus, however, does, though one woman in the FB group reported a safe vaginal delivery even suffering from LP)

Things that helped other women:
- from collated wisdom.

Borax baths: Though some were concerned about borax baths during pregnancy others found it was the best way to make everything feel good down there - and reported back on healthy births.
Instead of borax baths during pregnancy some opted for Baking soda (bicarbonate of soda) or Oatmeal baths or Epsom-salt baths, to soothe the itch.

Perineal massage - in the months prior to the birth, using oils, such as Bio-Oil, to soften and make stretchy the perineum (the most usual site for tears)

Many write of using creams and lotions including:
V magic ointment, coconut oil (with various infusions ie borax / lavender oil), small amounts of topical Estradiol, small amounts of topical CBD oil.

Ch 13: What to Wear or Use Down There

A) Underwear options: (ideas and options suggested by the collated wisdom of the group)

A lot of women choose to go commando and wear no underwear at all.

If going commando then a long skirt can work well – as do Hareem pants (trousers) as these have a low crotch so it doesn't cause chaffing.

Some women say going without underwear won't work for them because of having discharge or because of their creams and salves or that if they wear pants (trousers) or leggings without underwear, the clothing may rub and chafe the area.

Some women wear men's cotton boxers or underwear made for women that are like boxers - sometimes called 'boyfriend stretch shorties' or 'boy shorts'.

Some women wear men's underwear or buy underwear that is too big, so that they are loose fitting.

Underwear should allow your skin to breathe so that there is less irritation and damp held in the genital area.

Cotton is a naturally breathable material and so is a good choice from that perspective.
Some suggest that dyes used to colour underwear may irritate – others that the bleaching to make the cotton white may irritate.

You may have to experiment to see if either affect you – or see if you can get unbleached natural coloured cotton undies – which would then be an off-white shade.

There are some undies on the market made of bamboo – this is also very naturally breathable, lightweight and comfortable – but, like cotton, the processes to make it into a fibre require chemicals that may still linger and cause irritation to some women.

DermaSilk knickers (and other underwear) which is designed to be breathable and lightweight, has been recommended by some - though rather expensive it is used by people suffering from eczema too.

Washing your clothes:
Chemical residues can irritate your skin - here we have pointers, not products as they vary world-wide. It has been recommended that you avoid the 'bio' washing detergents. The 'bio' doesn't refer to biological or environmental - it usually mean it has a form of bleach in it to kill bacteria - so best avoided. Go instead for non-bio versions or simple soap detergents for your clothes - or no detergent at all and use eco-balls/wash balls.

B) Menstrual options: (ideas and options suggested by the collated wisdom of the group)

Tampons can be an irritant due to the chemicals used in their manufacture, as well as being painful on insertion for some when LS symptoms are very sore.

For some the lack of ‘wetness’ held close to their LS is one reason for sticking with tampons, as the wetness of the shed blood against their vulva can irritate some.

If using a tampon is too uncomfortable then there are other options.

The bleached white cotton-like/non-woven fibre in most popular brands of period-pads can irritate some women – so other alternatives have been sought.

Some women use natural brands like Naturacare or Veeda or 7th generation.

Some women use reusable cotton or flannel pads – either making them themselves or buying from a wide range of commercially made pads or from small home-based manufacturers selling on etsy and fb.

Some use a moon-cup - though finding one that is suitably flexible and fits into your vagina without trouble can be tricky. Ask for recommendations on one of the support groups.

Some use period-pants - like the cotton-based Thinx. Again, asking for recommendations is a good idea as they are not cheap initially - though once you are happy with your choice - your ‘set for your period’ will last you a long time.

Ch14: Problems concerning urination or defecation (peeing or pooping) - collated wisdom

#Problems concerning URINATION/ peeing

#1, Urine spraying everywhere – as the structure of the labia minora changes one of the problems people face is that the urine stream is no longer directed, and can even be mis-directed as a spray. This does two things, One, the urine hitting sore broken skin can sting, a lot, and Two, the urine spray lands on inner thighs, maybe even underclothes if not sufficiently lowered.

WHAT TO TRY:

Try keeping your knees together and leaning forward a bit. This means that your labia majora, pressed by your thighs, performs the urine directing job of the labia minora, and this can help direct a single stream directly into the toilet. It is rather counter-intuitive – as when we experience spray our natural inclination is to spread our thighs wider – which actually makes the spray-effect worse.

Try using a small disposable cup to direct the urine – and prevent it spraying onto your vulva or inner-thighs.

Place the cup just in-front of your urethra, and press the sides of the cup against your vulval area (if you are very sensitive you might want to lubricate the edges of the cup) This is as if you are going to pee into the cup – but as the cup is tipped the urine stream goes into and straight out of the cup – but your surrounding vulval area, etc, is protected from the urine – and the stream is directed into the toilet bowl. *{Method believed to be worked out by Barbara Bailey Zupan}*

#2 Stinging urethra and close surrounding area – but not spraying.

WHAT TO TRY:
Try making sure your urine is not so strong – drink the recommended amounts of liquid – your urine should be a light-straw colour. When it is diluted it is less strong and so does not sting as much - and only go when you really need to - so the stream is powerful.

Try coating your vulva and urethra with a barrier cream. Which one you choose is up to you. Coconut oil and borax will help *(see Ch 6 – section – 'with coconut oil')*, but some people prefer stickier, thicker creams such as made from castor oil *(see Ch 6 - section – 'without coconut oil')* or 'diaper/nappy cream' (zinc & castor oil cream) or even Vaseline *(but see Ch 11 section - External Triggers)*.

#3 Wiping dry after urination causes pain.

WHAT TO TRY:

Try NOT WIPING. The action of wiping seems to cause more pain, so try not to wipe.
'Rose-rolled' method: Taken that you are using a suitable soft-toilet paper, gather the sheets (4-5 will do) into a sort-of rose, holding the tight end together. Blot using the looser 'top' of this rose – so it is the edges that meet your vulval area, the touch is gentle and absorbs the urine evenly from all areas quickly.

You may need to do two 'roses' to be comfortably dry.

Try just making a pad of the toilet paper and patting gently.

Try only using toilet paper that is unbleached paper - as some of the treatments or dyes in toilet paper can cause stinging or reactions.

Try using a bamboo-based toilet paper, some find it softer.

Try not using toilet paper at all. Some ladies use wet-wipes - water only based ones – not with fragrances or containing other ingredients. {DO NOT FLUSH THESE – they will block up the sewers as they do not break down!}
Alternatively, some ladies have soft fabric cloths they keep for this purpose and wash after use.

Try using a bidet – or a bidet attachment to your toilet. This will wash away the urine, you still then need to blot dry. Many ladies find this very useful as it also deals with faecal elimination / defecation wiping too.

If you do not have these installed - or are out-and-about then....
Try a squirt (peri) bottle – many ladies like to have this filled with a borax solution to both wash away the urine and apply a mini borax soak – otherwise carry empty to fill and use as required. (see Ch 6).
(The **'CuloClean' top** transforms any old water/soda bottle into a squirt-bottle discreetly and cheaply)

After both of these methods you will probably still need to dry with your method of choice [Though some have said, at home they dry off with a hair-dryer!]

#Problems concerning DEFECATION / pooping

Many women have the classic 'figure 8' pattern of LS. This means that not only the vulva but also the perineum and the area all around the anus are affected. This often coincides with swelling that makes matters worse. Defecation (pooping) can therefore cause pain and fine fissures (skin splits).

#1 Some of this pain is made worse by wiping the excrement away with toilet paper.

(see problems with toilet paper above under #3)

WHAT TO TRY:

Try using a bidet – or a bidet attachment to your toilet to wash away all the excrement – then pat dry with toilet paper (*see above for paper to avoid and 'rose' method)

If you do not have these installed - or are out-and-about then....

Try removing the majority of the excrement without rubbing the skin with the paper – then washing the remaining excrement away down the toilet using a plastic squirt bottle*, or water bottle adapted with a 'CuloClean' top (*See Ch. 6). This can be carried empty and filled as required to just squirt the area clean (always 'front towards the back'). Use 'rose-rolled' toilet-paper or just folded as a pad, to dry and check on cleanliness.

Ch 15: Lichen Sclerosus in MEN & Notes on LS in Children

When we first hear of LS, we are often told only that it is only pre-puberty and post menopausal women who get LS - the doctors often forget to mention that not only does this occur in women *within* their reproductive years – but **it also occurs in men and boys.**

In men it is sometimes given a different name: balanitis xerotica obliterans (BXO) - but it is actually the same condition.

Where it occurs in men:

It occurs mainly on the penis, causing severe problems, and, less frequently, around the anus as well in some men.

Description

Balanitis Xerotica Obliterans (BXO) (LS in Men) is a chronic, often progressive disease, which can lead to phimosis (restriction of the foreskin so it can't pull back) and urethral stenosis (covering the exit hole of the penis giving urination problems like retention) affecting both urinary and sexual function.

Just the same as LS in women it is not catching (contagious), it is not a sexually transmitted disease (STD) and it is painful - but it is rarer than LS in women.

Usual treatments:

Steroid creams are usually the first-line treatment but have a limited role and surgical intervention is frequently necessary. The usual surgical procedure (circumcision) is often preferred in the first instance - with the premise that recurrence of disease will require a more definitive reconstruction.

Some doctors seem to suggest that removal of the foreskin (circumcision) cures the man of LS. However, from reports from men – it seems this is not so, it may alleviate the problem initially but the LS returns - and still affects the glans, with white plaques or thin, cracking, sore skin - exacerbated by friction. It may also progress down the shaft and affect the anal area. Having LS can make sex extremely painful as the skin can be very delicate.

Borax protocols and information:
[see chapters 4, 5 & 6]
Treatment with borax soaks seem to help give relief to men as much as with women. It is to be noted that starting low and increasing the borax slowly is just as important for men as women. (we have seen a tendency in men to think 'the more the better' and go with the maximum amounts from the start – which is not necessarily the best way to instigate any new treatment)

If choosing to ingest – the measurements of borax given in Ch 6 in the high dose protocol should not be exceeded.
Though men **of a heavier build** using the maintenance dose protocol should take 2-4 teaspoons of the maintenance solution a day (as opposed to 1-2 for most women)

There are LS support groups specifically for men, and a few LS groups that are open to both men and women

- including one set up by Allicia - because this got the conversation going better - For Loved Ones: **A Group Of Sharing About A Loved One With Lichen Sclerosus.**

See Appendix 2: You Are Not Alone - for details of other support information.

Notes on LS in Children:

It is most distressing and frustrating to be the parent of a child with LS. The treatment and help for children is as weak and patchy as it is for adults, with the added problems of even more than usual misdiagnosis (even terrible accusations).
The fact that the parent cannot actually know what the child is experiencing, but must be the mediator with the medical fraternity, is also a difficulty.

From Allicia's FB group (see p.100) for parents of children suffering with LS, it appears that the Borax bathing protocols help ease the itching the most (start low and work up).
Diet is also very important in helping these young ones get comfortable, especially with regard to checking how the main flare-trigger foods affect them, and eliminating the culprits from their diet.
Supporting a good gut-biome is also important, maybe doing a top-up with a good multi-strain probiotic then eating foods to support the good bacteria, especially if there is any reason to believe it has been compromised by medication or infections.
All the chapters about food choices, clothes, salves, toilet-paper, etc are also relevant to children.
Note: Many children 'grow out' of their LS when puberty kicks in - though it may return later in life.

Ch 16: Commercial Lotions and Potions

(these suggestions and comments are from the collated wisdom from the support group - mentioning them does ***not*** *endorse them as our personal recommendation)*

As well as the Homemade salves and cremes shared in Chapter 6 – some ladies have found some commercial products helpful – do your own research into their ingredients – as you will know which chemicals you can tolerate and which ones you cannot.

In alphabetical order:

Aquaphor: *Used by some as an alternative to Vaseline Petroleum Jelly. Good to use as a moisturizer and good for soothing discomfort. Some use it as a barrier for swimming. (contains petrolatum, mineral oil and lanolin)*

Calmoseptine: *This is good for fissures and very good for anal Lichen Sclerosus. It makes a good barrier cream and has a menthol cooling feel to it. Some love the cooling feeling but some think it is too strong.*

Carolla's Beeswax Skin Cream: *A thick moisturiser that is good to use as a barrier. Good for dryness and fissures. (contains beeswax – and borax!!)*

Colloidal Silver: *use in gel form - for helping fine cuts heal.*

Country Comfort Herbal Savvy: *A good inexpensive herbal salve for healing of fissures and sores.*

Emuaid: *Very healing and soothing. Provides a cooling feeling that most like, but a few feel uncomfortable with the cooling feeling. Contains emu oil, which is highly recommended for moisturising for Lichen Sclerosus.*

Comes in two strengths, blue (for LS) and red (emuaidMax). (contains colloidal silver and emu oil - taken as a by-product of the emu meat trade)

Emu Oil: *Purified Emu Oil - applied as it is.*

Egyptian Magic: *A very popular skin cream used by celebrities. This is used for all type of skin disorders. Contains a lot of natural bee products. (contains bee products – wax/honey/royal jelly/propolis)*

Estriol cream: *Used to treat vulvar atrophy. This deals with hormones, so make sure that you contact your doctor. This can be bought without a prescription.*

Hempvana cream: *This is a pain relieving cream. It isn't used a lot, but a few people have had success with it.*

Julva: *Helps keep moisture in, builds the skin and also for atrophy. This is marketed towards menopausal women. This was developed by an ob/gyn. It has DHEA (Dehydroepiandrosterone), which is a steroid hormone made by the adrenal glands, that acts on the body much like testosterone and is converted into testosterone and oestrogen. (Also contains emu-oil)*

Lazarus naturals: *This is a cream with CBD that some have had success with healing.*

Lisepten salves: *This comes in a salve, cream, oil and a serum. There are variations of it with coconut oil or jojoba. This is a very popular choice that a lot of women love. It is created by a woman that has Lichen Sclerosus. Very healing and helps with dryness. Some people report that it stains your underwear and clothes.*

Organic Magic Balm: *Good for chafed dry skin. Made out of natural oils.*

Perrin Naturals Cream: *Advertised specifically for Lichen Sclerosus. Heals and moisturises. Some don't care for the strong smell and a couple of people stated that it stings open sores. Overall, seems to be a popular choice.*

St. Francis Red Clover Plus Salve: *Helps with soreness and itchiness and is reported to have a thick consistency like Vaseline. It is reported to have a strong herbal smell.*

Terrasil: *This is used for skin repair. Can be used to heal fissures and sores.*

Vmagic: *Good option for moisturizing for dryness. It also works well for reducing inflammation.*

Ch 17: Skin condition terms it is useful to know

Alphabetical list:

Bacterial Vaginosis {BV}: A condition of an overgrowth of bacteria in the vagina that has a foul odour and has a white discharge. It can be itchy and cause painful urination.

Balanitis Xerotica Obliterans {BXO}: Lichen Sclerosus in Men is often called this.

Chronic Vulvar Candidiasis: A reoccurring itching and discharge from a yeast infection.

Epidermolysis bullosa: All forms of epidermolysis bullosa cause fluid-filled skin blisters to develop in response to injuries that don't normally warrant that type of reaction. For example, gentle rubbing of the skin or even an increase in room temperature can cause blisters to form.

Herpes Genital {HSV-2}: A sexually transmitted infection that causes itching and sores on the genitalia.

Herpes simplex {HSV-1}: This is the herpes that causes cold sores.

Human Papilloma Virus {HPV}: A sexually transmitted infection that causes warts on the genitalia. Also linked to the development of cancer.

Interstitial Cystitis: A painful condition in the bladder causes increase in urination and painful sex.

Lichen Planus {LP}: A skin disease that is similar to Lichen Sclerosus with inflammation and lesions and can also be inside the vagina. Also has an 'oral' version {OLP} which occurs in the mouth.

Lichen Sclerosus {LS}: A skin disease that causes white thinning skin that tears and bruises easily on the genitals and the anal areas.
A fuller description: Lichen sclerosis is a common skin condition in women and usually affects the vulva (entrance to the vagina) or anus. There are no known causative agents. Lotions, soaps or perfumes cannot be blamed and it is not caused by any bacteria, virus or sexual activity.
It is probably an auto-immune condition. This means that your own antibodies cause a biological reaction in certain areas of skin and the result is inflammation.
Eventually, continued inflammation causes the skin to become thin. In severe cases the lips surrounding the vagina (called labia) begin to stick together and can bury the clitoris - this is called fusing. The skin can tear easily but will heal again but can cause scar tissue.
The inflammation causes itching, especially at night. The natural impulse is to scratch. Unfortunately relief from scratching is temporary and scratching causes more inflammation and further itching.
Established lichen sclerosis is not curable. The itching or soreness is variable and depends on the degree of inflammation. Treatment is to reduce the inflammation and make the symptoms more bearable. Adapted from a NHS website

Lichen Simplex Chronicus {LSC}: A skin condition of Lichen Sclerosus when the skin gets thickened from constant scratching/damage.

Psoriasis: White dry flaky skin that burns and itches. It can be found on multiple places on the body.

Scleroderma: A localized form of scleroderma results in patches of thickened skin, while systemic scleroderma is the form that has the greatest impact on people's lives, affecting muscles and organs.

Vitiligo: A disorder that can cause white skin patches similar to those of LS. Vitiligo can occur together with LS.

VSN: Vulvar Squamous Neoplasia: A benign, precancerous, or malignant, neoplasm that arises from the squamous epithelium of the vulva.

VIN: Vulvar Intraepithelial Neoplasia: Changes in the vulvar skin that is considered precancerous. It is not cancer, but could develop into cancer.

Vulvodynia: Is a general term used for unexplained pain in the vaginal area.

***

Bartholin Cyst: Not a 'skin condition' but something people sometimes query on the support site, especially when they find a swelling that affects the vulva.

The Bartholin's glands are a pair of glands between the vagina and the vulva. A **cyst** can sometimes affect the labia majora - you may feel a soft, painless lump. One side may look swollen or bigger than usual. This does not usually cause any problems. But if the cyst grows very large, you may feel pain in the skin surrounding the vagina. Visit your doctor, the problem can usually be treated easily.

Ch 18: LS and other Auto Immune conditions

You won't get far into any LS support group before you notice than many of us suffer, or have suffered, from at least one other auto-immune condition (this assuming that you accept LS is an auto-immune). So if this is you - you are not alone - and it may be that the initial problem was the same trigger. It has been said that if you suffer from one auto immune disorder you are likely to develop another one – unless you can deal with the trigger. Whether this is a disrupted gut-biome, allowing the invasion of inflammatory molecules into the blood stream, or an undetected case of Lyme's disease, or major trauma / stress, or different triggers - is very much an individual thing and as such only you will know where it all began. Whether that very same thing will cause an auto-immune in someone else is down to each person's own genetic make-up – and there is evidence that this vulnerability to developing an auto-immune when the trigger is encountered can, therefore, be hereditary.

Here's a list of other Auto-immune conditions (or strongly-linked-to-auto-immune-conditions^) mentioned in LS support groups. **Alphabetically:** Adhesive capsulitis^ (*frozen-shoulder*) - Allopecia – Asthma – Bechet's - Coeliac – Colitis – Crohns – Diabetes (*Type 1*) – Endometriosis^ - Fibromyalgia - Graves(*hyperthyroidism*) - Hashimotos (*hypothyroidism*) – IBS (*irritable bowel syndrome*) - Lupus – Melasma^ - Morphea (*localised scleroderma*)- PCOS^ (*polycystic ovary syndrome*) - Psoriasis – Raynauds syndrome^ - Rheumatoid Arthritis – Sarcoidosis – Scleroderma – Sjogren's syndrome – Vasculitis – Vitiligo

APPENDIX 1

Where in the world to buy borax

Borax is also known as sodium borate, sodium tetraborate, or disodium tetraborate.

A list from collated wisdom

- so just the ones we've heard about

Do NOT buy a borax *substitute*

(Alphabetically by Country)

Australia at Woolworths or Coles called Bare Essentials Borax or Blants online.
Canada - see USA below.
Denmark - from a Blacksmith.
Dubai - from Ace stores.
Finland eBay for the UK.
Ireland at Bomar Aromatherapy online bomar.ie
Mexico at hardware stores.
Netherlands adam@bluebayaquatics.co.uk (will ship)
New Zealand at a pharmacy/chemist, bulk food store/ gardening or farming supplies. Bunnings. Binn Inn. Trademe online, Pharmacydirect online.
Spain La Mezcla Perfecta and Drogueria Manuel Riesago.
Sweden online at Pronatu.com
United States and **Canada** you can buy 20 Mule Borax at any grocery store or any store that sells laundry products, or on Amazon.
U.K. adam@bluebayaquatics.co.uk, Trade Chem online, Baldwin's Chemist online, Reidsuk on ebay.co.uk

APPENDIX 2

YOU ARE NOT ALONE!

Support groups, websites, blogs – a list of places to find help *(current for print date)*

Unfortunately things on the internet are not always where they were - even last week.
This is, as you will know, why we have made this book – as this should remain in place and available to those who need it.

However, we have compiled this list in the hope that you will find good, friendly and kind online support, information and understanding in the places we have indicated – we will endeavour to keep this section updated on a new-edition basis.

Search for the terms in bold

Ann's blog posts around Lichen Sclerosus. **AnnFoweraker.com/category/lichen-Sclerosus-ls/**

Allicia's Facebook pages – ***search in Facebook:***
For Women: **Sharing is Caring about Lichen Sclerosus et al**
For Loved Ones: **A Group Of Sharing About A Loved One With Lichen Sclerosus**

For parents of **children** with LS: **A Group Of Sharing About Children With Lichen Sclerosus**

Search on the new **MeWe** - social friendship site for Allicia's **MeWe** page: **Sharing is Caring about Lichen Sclerosus et al** *(& Join this back-up group too !)*

Fabia Brackenbury FB: **World Lichen Sclerosus Day January 17**
Jan 17th - A good day to raise awareness about LS!

Jaqueline Grimsley's UK FB:
Lichen Sclerosus UK Natural Support Group

Linda Larkin's FB: **Lichen Sclerosis & Lichen Planus Skin Disorder Support**

Amy Mangis' FB: **Lichen Sclerosis / Sclerosus; Healing naturally through nourishment**

Annie McGee's FB: **Lichen Sclerosis Support Group**

Romana Nova's FB: **Your Lichen Sclerosis Solution**

Website links - For your information:

Fabia Brackenbury: **LichenSclerosus.org**

EARTHCLINIC:
earthclinic.com/remedies/borax/

LIFESAVINGHEALTH:
lifesavinghealth.org/how-do-you-cure-lichen-sclerosus-naturally-heres-how.html

The Borax Conspiracy - mentioned in this book **health-science-spirit.com/borax.htm** *(this is the website by Walter Last)* the article can be found here and is re-posted elsewhere.

If you found this book helpful please remember to review and share - thank you

For Your Own Notes:

Printed in Great Britain
by Amazon

68427603R00059